DIKSHA AT ST. MARTIN'S

DIKSHA AT ST. MARTIN'S

SIDDHARTH CHOWDHURY

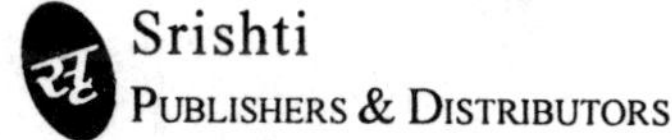

SRISHTI PUBLISHERS & DISTRIBUTORS
64-A, Adhchini
Sri Aurobindo Marg
New Delhi 110 017
srishtipublishers@forindia.com

First published by SRISHTI PUBLISHERS & DISTRIBUTORS in 2002

Rs. 145.00
ISBN 81-87075-98-8

Cover design by Vinayak Bhattacharya

To

Patna

Contents

Acknowledgement

I would like to thank the editors of *Debonair, The Brown Critique* and the *Tehelka Literary Review* where most of these stories in a slightly altered form were first published. To my parents for their unflinching support to a wayward son. My brother Sanjay for keeping a well stocked Bar. My sister-in-law for letting me use it. My young philanthropic nephew Sreyash for finally deciding not to feed the manuscript to the neighour's Doberman Pinscher. In the end Pragya – muse, lover, comrade, wife – for believing all my lies.

HOMEWARD BOUND

It was just before Dushera and the schools were closed in Patna. The oppressive heat of September had given way to the lazy warmth of October. The evenings had grown cooler than before. Javed Ahmed Siddiqui, a high school teacher, was going home to Gaya. He boarded the 6.45 Passenger to Gaya from platform no. 3 and settled down to a seat near the window. The familiar smell of fresh hot shit and stale vinegary urine assailed his nostrils. The train started on its way. It was dark outside now and as the train left the city limits, the scent of wildflowers mixed with ganja wafted in with the cool air. He liked the rush of wind on his face. He was an ordinary sort of a man. A contemplative man. A man who was more often than not happy and perhaps for that reason alone a rare kind of a man. He looked forward to the week's holiday to be spent with his family. Parents, brothers and sisters, assorted nephews and nieces. Whenever he went home, the children wouldn't leave him alone even for a minute. They crowded around him all the time and tagged along with him everywhere. He would play cricket with them in the mornings and in the evenings tell them stories of all kind for he had a fantastic imagination and recite for their benefit couplets of Ghalib most of which he knew by heart. Most important of all he never asked them to study. A rare and ever endearing quality in any uncle. He taught urdu and persian at a missionary school in Patna. At 35 he had a receeding hairline and an aquiline nose of a mughal warrior and laugh lines had started appearing around his mouth. He had the beginnings of a double chin. Till a couple of years back his parents were anxious to see him married but he knew he couldn't afford a wife. At the same time he realised that some things would become much easier, if he just said yes. Sex for one. Food for two. He felt he should settle down, have a couple of kids, a regular family but he had one curious notion. He didn't want his wife to be a poor man's wife. He didn't want his bride to have the same slow stagnant life of his mother and sisters. A life of low compromises and nil delights. An apparently stable slow lower middle class existence with a tentative hold on respectability. An inch away from poverty always.

He had plans for his begum. He wanted to be affluent enough to buy gifts for her whenever he wanted to: perfume, silk and gold. Meanwhile time was running out. He had saved some money but time was running out. He would probably say yes if asked again, he thought to himself all the time staring into the still darkness of the hurtling countryside. They hadn't asked again in over a year. He wondered whether his parents would ask again.

He wondered what Mirza Ghalib would have done in a similar situation but then he said to himself 'Now that's a thought. A crazy thought. He was a rebel, wasn't he? He was a genius. How can one compare oneself to Ghalib? You can't compare yourself to Ghalib. He could do anything. If he wanted to marry someone, he would just marry her, simple. He surely wouldn't let a petty thing like poverty stop him from doing what he wanted to do. He was touched by God. He could run a gambling den in his own house. Kill a man if the need arose and then go home and write poetry so sublime that it would make the dead live again. He was a hero and heroes can do anything. You are not a hero.'

The train chugged along on the familiar tracks past the villages and small kasbas indifferent in its battered majesty.

He wondered what it felt like to be a poet, a regular genius, to be able to change people's lives and their world with the words they write in the sanctuary of their lonely rooms. To weave words like pearls on a string to adorn a beloved's graceful neck and sometimes like a stone in the slingshot to shatter the narrow mirror in which society sees its reflection and preens in delight. What heady feeling it must excite to be able to wield such powers. But it was of a past era he was thinking about and he knew that no one read poets anymore except other poets. Even Javed hadn't read any of the younger poets except Javed Akhtar but then even he was primarily a lyricist. Javed's point of reference was of 40-50 years past, the time of Firaq Gorakhpuri and Sahir Ludhianwi and Kaifi Azmi, the revolutionary poets of the forties and fifties. Those were his heroes but there was only one God and that was Ghalib for him. What made Ghalib what he was? What made him tick? He wished he had been born in the last century and had known Ghalib. He was sure he would have been a friend of Ghalib's. He said to himself, 'The similarity between me and Ghalib is that of the Tomcat and the Tiger. Only the Genus is same. He was a poet and a prophet. Sometimes drunk sometimes dangerous but always generous. As adept with a rapier as with a quill walking the bylanes of Chandni Chowk with the cool swagger of a local hero. Tortured yet brimming with life. Sunshine and despair. A walking contradiction. He would have been a hard man to love but I would have loved him. I would have been his friend.'

Javed smiled to himself as he thought about this. He wanted to write a detailed biography of Ghalib and had been taking notes for the past two years. Mirza Ghalib was a kind of a obsession for him. For him everything that was there to celebrate in life was right there in Ghalib's poetry, in his couplets and ghazals and one only had to dunk his mind for couple of minutes everyday and have his jaded spirits rise up rejuvenated in no time at all. He sometimes dreamt of Ghalib in his long achkan and cap walking with him through some gali and they would enter a haveli after a while and then start climbing the stairs of a winding staircase. Ghalib in front leading Javed by the hand but the stairs would go on and on forever and then it would be morning and he would wake up. Now as he sat in the train looking out of the window the recollection of that dream – it was always that same dream – made him laugh out involuntarily.

He heard a girl giggle and he looked out of the corner of his eye and saw a girl of 16-17 sitting opposite him diagonally, suppressing her giggles with her dupatta and having a hard time doing it. For a second Javed was surprised that there were others beside him. He had been totally engrossed in his reveries. He was embarrassed then. A middle aged man in a dhoti kurta who was sitting beside her looked at him and then said something to the girl. She looked at Javed and quietened down. The giggles subsided. The other passengers too checked out Javed with some interest and then looked away. This chronic day dreaming had always landed him in sticky situations. The girl probably thinks that I am crazy or something but she is so pretty she can think anything she likes and as he mused about this he smiled some more but then he realised what he was doing and he stopped quickly.

The compartment was filled to capacity and some of the passengers were squatting in the aisle itself. At the end of the compartment near the gate, three armed railway policemen stood around smoking. They all confirmed to a type – large, potbellied and sluggish looking. A family of four was sitting besides Javed. The father in a Khadi kurta pajama with a badge of green wheel insignia pinned to the breast, looked like a grassroot level political worker. He was close-eyed with a small nose and luxuriant moustache whose ends he chewed with his tobacco stained teeth constantly. He had the face of a minor extortionist and the blustery rude behaviour to go with it. With him were his wife who was in ghungat and who kept quiet all the time and a little girl of 10 or 11 to whom none of the parents paid much attention to and then there was the son the crown prince who was a voluble little fellow of around four years and who talked and shouted and sang and in whom the parents delighted entirely. He sang songs from hindi movies and the girl who had giggled at Javed found it to be very endearing but Javed felt otherwise. The favourite song of the kid was the popular 'I love my India' from the Subhash Ghai movie *Pardes*. He sang it once and then at the insistence of the girl did an encore and then again and again. Javed said to himself in dismay that probably his nephews would do the same to him when he reached home in a couple of hours time.

Across from Javed, on the side of the aisle, sat couple of young men in their early twenties. They talked among themselves most of the time. Once in a while they would fall silent and watch the other passengers. One of them with a thin smeary little moustache kept looking at the girl. As was mentioned earlier the girl was pretty. In the first bloom of youth and aware of her prettiness and sure of the fact that what she had was something rare perhaps transient but while it lasted life itself would on bended knees do her very bidding. Once in a while Javed stole a glance at her and wished that she would look at him again. She was fair and had a sharp little nose with a silver nathani embedded in her left nostril and a generous mouth and light coloured eyes that twinkled with mischief and a certain vibrant joy in being alive, taking in everything with a gaze that was both inquisitive and bold but it was her breasts, her left breast actually, that captivated Javed. Under the tight kurta and partly uncovered from the sides by the dupatta, side wise curved from her armpit to the folds of the dupatta, a mound of solid jelly slung low. Would she have brown areolae or pink ones? Pink nipples of course, she was so fair with tiny light coloured hair around the areolae almost invisible with her skin. If he could just touch them, squeeze them softly, roll the nipple around with his tongue. Ah heaven. Look at me. The girl looked at him straight on at that moment and he was startled. He turned his head towards the window hurriedly. Would she know what he was thinking? If on this visit his parents asked him to marry he would definitely say yes. This can't go on he said to himself. Could she see it in his face? He was getting to be like an adolescent each passing day. The girl probably thinks that I am another of those middle aged lechers but I am not middle aged. I am only 35. My god I am 35!

The girl wasn't thinking any of those things about Javed. She wasn't even aware that he was checking out her breasts. The left one in particular but she was acutely aware of his presence. She thought him to be interesting and funny. When he would stare out of the window all kinds of expressions would glide across his face like silver white fishes in a dark pool. He was like one of the actors in the Ramleela troupe that visited her village every year during durga puja. May be he is an actor too but ... he doesn't look poor enough. He is too 'tip-top' for that. He would be just right for the role of Sita though, his mouth is so pretty and she giggled some more. If she had known that he was a Muslim she would have been mortified. Muslims were dangerous. They were unclean. Muslims were bad news. Her father whispered to her in Bhojpuri to keep quite and then glared at Javed again who was as usual looking out of the window. The soft prettiness of the girl, her close proximity, the smell of woodsmoke in the air, coupled with the fact that he was homeward bound had made his mind segue into a mellow poetic mode. The long stretching darkness with the occasional night fire dancing in them like fireflies in a dark room seemed to him like a simile for his own whole life with its routine everyday compromises and fugitive desires and it was passing him by in a hurry.

He wondered what Ghalib would think about the simile. Would he use it in a couplet? Probably not, he decided after a while.

The train reached Nadaul and some people got off and a group of five youngmen in their early twenties or late teens bordered the coach. After a five-minute halt the train resumed its journey and the trouble started just after that.

The young men whipped out kattas and they were joined by those two men who were sitting opposite Javed. Couple of them covered the policemen who were taken by surprise and they didn't put up a fight. The policemen handed over their rifles. Rest of the men started looting the passengers systematically. Nobody protested or said anything but handed over whatever valuables they had. It was the third robbery in as many weeks in that line alone. 1997 would prove to be a banner year for train robberies in Bihar. Javed felt as if a small cube of ice had suddenly been lodged above his left cheekbones and now the intense fear that he could feel rise up in waves inside his heart made the ice melt into little droplets which coursed down the side of his face, inside the skin. The little boy was quiet now, wide eyes staring into terror ridden eyes of his close eyed father. He had never seen him so pale and submissive before and it awed him. He did no more encores of 'I love my India.'

Javed could see the terror all around him reflected in the

faces and eyes of his fellow passengers. They all looked alike. They looked trapped but there was no anger in their eyes just empty despair which paralysed them totally.

Javed felt that if he stood up he would just sink to the floor in a squelchy mass of muscles, blood and bone. An open sluice of water was running from his knee caps to his feet. 'Coward' his mind whispered back to him. As he handed over his wallet and watch he could see his hand shake uncontrollably. The man who took his wallet and watch laughed and it went like a spike through Javed's ear. It was the man with the thin smeary moustache and shifty eyes. He didn't appear much older than many of his senior class fellows Javed noted. 'Coward' his mind screamed back. He felt ashamed with himself and a tiny flame of anger started flickering up in his breast. He was not a fighting man, had always shied away from confrontations of any kind but today he wished otherwise. He wished he were different. He wished he wasn't such a coward. The slow flame of anger burned higher and higher but he didn't do anything. Anger warmed him up and he felt better. The ice was gone from underneath the skin. Something like this had happened to him only once before, on a chilly early December evening in 1992. He had felt the same kind of terror and isolation of being completely alone. He hadn't gone to his school for days after that. He felt like he didn't have a single friend left. There wasn't anyone he could trust anymore. He had taken it personally then and he took it personally now.

The dacoits looted in a leisurely fashion. They abused when they felt like, slapped the men around a little just for fun and touched the woman. Everyone stared down to the floor. No one raised their voices. No body protested. No one tried to fight. The policemen now divested of their rifles and with it their duty were feeling relieved. They huddled together smoking and whispering among themselves.

Looting over, one of the dacoits pulled the chain and the train started slowing down. The thin mustachioed man who was their leader now suddenly caught hold of the girl and started dragging her towards the gate. The girl didn't shout and she didn't cry. She just didn't do anything. Her father too looked on helplessly. He was so frightened that when he tried to speak he just couldn't form the necessary words. All the other passengers looked down to the floor. It is always the recollection of the immediate past during moments of crisis, the way things were just couple of hours back, that fuels the terror and it was that terror which reduced the other passengers from healthy vibrant organism who could sense and feel to the level of soul dead Zombies. They were lucky. It could have been their own sisters, wives, daughters but miraculously it wasn't and they were lucky. They didn't want any part in it. They didn't want their lucks to change. If they only closed their eyes and kept quiet, the nightmare would be over in minutes and then they could pretend that it never happened. Afterwards with a sigh of relief they could resume their journeys and their lives.

A silent scream rose in Javed's heart, a scream like that of a small furry animal in great pain, as he saw the girl being dragged. His mind felt like something dank and dirty, a rotten smelling jelly like creature had suddenly attached itself to it and was sucking out memory, love, past pleasure away from him like a virus and leaving everything blank beneath. He grew calm in the few seconds that had elapsed and he realised what he would do. He didn't feel any terror anymore but only the sense of being intrinsically violated. He could see to the immediate future with great lucidity now and what he saw there didn't deter him from doing what he was now determined to do.

The train had slowed down considerably and was now coming to a halt when Javed said calmly to the man, 'You have got what you wanted. Don't take the girl. Please leave her alone.' In reply the man squeezed her breasts and abused her and then said to Javed 'Saàle Hero banta hai, maaar do saale ko'. There was silence all around. The girl looked at Javed and he realised he didn't even know her name. Not that it mattered anymore. One of the dacoits put his katta at point blank range and shot Javed through his heart and then pushed him back to his berth. The girl screamed then. A thin piercing knife like cry. The train lurched then and stopped. The man released the girl, pushed her away and then scrambled towards the gate in great hurry. In a few seconds all the dacoits had got down. They left the rifles on the ground and then disappeared into the vast darkness. The policemen got down and collected their rifles. The girl slumped down to the floor and fainted. In a few minutes the train started to move again. Meanwhile the father went forward and picked his girl up, relief written all over the face and moved towards the gate where the policemen were standing. The girl had started coming to her senses.

The girl pointed towards Javed with her finger and looked into her father's eyes but he didn't do anything. All the other passengers picked up their baggage and moved towards the gate on both the sides. They all wanted to move away as fast and far away as possible from the sight of Javed slumped head down on his chest slowly painfully dying. He was like a dead rat in Surat in the time of the plague. Even the sight of him would contaminate them. They didn't want any part in it. They had already erased him from their memory. They would never talk about it to anyone. Crisis now over, denial had set in. They were all honest hardworking men and women, bourgeoise, petit bourgeoise. The common people. They were respectable people and they didn't want any part in it. They were right too.

JAVED? As life slowly ebbed away drop by drop he thought how utterly stupid his life had turned out to be. It was not despair just a simple realization. He was in terrible pain and was barely conscious now. He saw the familiar dream unfolding before his eyes and with greater clarity than ever before. He was walking beside Ghalib down one of the galies of Ballimaran and both of them were silent and they came to the familiar haveli with its weather beaten façade but inside it was clean and cool and they started to climb the stairs but somehow it was narrow, steep and straight now while earlier it had been a winding staircase. Ghalib led him by the hand. There was a room at the end of it which was not there before and they entered the room. A clean and bare but well lighted room and there was large bed in the middle of the room with a large green sheet spread on it. Javed lay down on the bed and Ghalib sat on the edge looking at him and smiling broadly. Javed closed his eyes. When he opened them again, there was no one around. He was all alone. He died then.

As the train reached Jehanabad station, all the passengers got off and boarded other compartments. The policemen got down too. In a little while another group of policemen arrived and they took away the body.

The girl wanted to see whether Javed was alive or not but her father who was now openly crying slapped her hard and dragged her down from the coach. He would forget everything. He would forget that a man had molested his daughter right before his eyes and he couldn't do a thing, that another man had tried to save her and was shot in return. He would forget that he had refused to help that man. He would forget everything.

One month later. Early one evening the girl made dinner, served her two younger brothers and then went to her father's room and locked the door. Her mother was in the kitchen. Father hadn't come home yet. She tied her dupatta to the ceiling fan. She tugged it hard to see if it would hold. Then she put a stool on the bed, climbed up and tied the lower end of the dupatta to her neck. She kicked off the stool. Her fingers were clenched into fists.

SERAPHIM AND CHERUBIM

Hriday K. Seraphim was the 6-B class monitor. A uniformly bright and popular lad who was also a keen cricketer. A bona-fide future pillar of society. The right stuff. Being the class monitor was yet the most spectacular achievement of his young life. But it was also the source of his secret pain, one he couldn't share with anybody. Not even his parents. One, which gnawed at his self-worth like a rat and left it, tattered each passing night.

The reason, rather the man behind the reason being Adrian E.Cherubim. The new class teacher who was also the stopgap moral-science tutor. Cherubim, a slight young man in his early thirties, not very bright and with not much of a prospect for marriage except perhaps with a passing adivasi servant girl, loved cute, well- groomed young boys from clean- cut families, definitely below the age of thirteen, who wouldn't put a compass in his eye while he nibbled their succulent ears.

For Cherubim, the old bugger, it was love at first sight. The first time he saw Hriday, during roll- call, he knew that the present year at this new school in the Gangetic plains with its mock gothic depressive exterior would turn out to be his *Annus Mirabilis*. That very evening he contrived to keep Hriday back after school. He announced he needed a volunteer for an act of profound piety. He needed a boy who could transcribe a passage each from the Bible, the *Gita,* and the Koran dealing with the virtues of pure and austere life on to the black board for the next morning's moral science lesson. Of course, nobody volunteered. Children are not stupid. They only seem so at times.

'For God and Country' thundered Cherubim at the tousle –haired and shifty eyed congregation. 'Isn't that suppose to be our motto. Well, you are too young to do anything for your country, except perhaps collectively to go to the "toilet" on it, granted. But remember one is never too young to do anything for God. Since nobody has volunteered, we must shut our eyes and pray, while I confer with the Almighty as to who will do his work today.'

After a minute Cherubim gently opened his eyes, smiled beatifically and said 'Hriday K. Seraphim'. The next day Hriday was made the class monitor. For a couple of weeks after that Cherubim left Hriday alone. But soon he was back to his old ways and would frequently ask Hriday to stay after school time to do 'God's humble work'. Hriday had never thought that the innocuous looking legend 'For God and Country' which was printed on the crest of all his shirts, and one which he had treated with exemplary indifference suddenly acquire fangs so sharp that each morning, as he would put it on, he could feel it burrow deep into his heart and deposit drops of poison in his blood. Half the time he would be in a daze. He didn't know what was happening to him anymore. But whatever it was it wasn't good. It made him sick. He thought about telling his parents but the shame … He blamed himself. He must have done something wrong. He couldn't concentrate on anything. The studies suffered and from a charming outgoing personality, his became a morose and silent one. Couple of months went by. The first-term exams approached. Hriday started resisting. He wouldn't heed God's call anymore. When the results came out, Hriday had failed for the first time in his life in History/Civics/Geography. Needless to add Cherubim was the teacher who was assigned this paper. His parents were shocked but Hriday knew he couldn't tell them ever. For the moment he only concentrated on the fact that the approaching summer vacation would effectively put him out of reach of his nemesis. Perhaps by the time the vacation ended there would be a new candidate to do God's work. 'Please let it be Ritwik. He is such an arsehole. He might even enjoy it.' Hriday prayed fervently.

But God, as we all convent-educated buggers know, like Elvis moves in mysterious ways. A day before the vacation Hriday's father informed him that Mr. Cherubim would come thrice a week during the holidays to tutor him in History/ Civics/Geography, with an additional lesson thrown in on moral science on the second Sundays.

'That nice young man himself came to my office and offered his services. He said you have much untapped potential, though looking at you I wonder what made him say that. He said he would do it for free but of course I refused. Judging by his clothes he could sure use the money.'

Talk about one's worst nightmare coming true. Now one wasn't even safe in one's own home anymore. Again he blamed himself. If he only hadn't spurned Cherubim's advances things wouldn't have come to such a sorry pass. All night long he thought about it and by morning he had reconciled himself to a compromise. He would meet Mr. Cherubim and be the obedient lad he earlier was, in return he should be spared during the vacations. The thought of Cherubim in his own home nauseated him.

'Come to the auditorium after four and we will solve your problem.' Cherubim said to him during the lunch break with a wink so manic that it almost looked like a muscle disorder. By three all the 'goodbyes' for the vacation had been said and the school was practically empty. By four it was empty, except for Osta the ancient watchman in his perch by the portico, who couldn't keep awake even in mid-day.

The auditorium was at one end of the school. By the side of the dark pond. A full ten minutes walk from the main building. With bowed head and drooping shoulders, tie askew, like a man condemned, Hriday shuffled towards his fate. The door of the auditorium was ajar and on the ledge inside, the big padlock with the key, stuck out of its groove like a thermometer, was kept. It was dark but the light of the green room was switched on. Suddenly the fog in his mind cleared. The last drop of poison kicked in. A deceptively simple thought occurred to Hriday. He went upto the green room and cautiously peeked in. Yes Cherubim was there, reading Dale Carnegie's *How to Win Friends and Influence People*; a book he carried everywhere around with him. Smug and at peace with the world.

Hriday quickly switched off the light and bolted the door. He locked the main door of the auditorium with a calmness that had all but disappeared from his persona. By the time he crossed the dark pond, the screams had grown fainter. He stopped and turned, with all the lung he could put into it, shouted 'For God and Country' against the wind, and flung the key into the weed choked pond. Then with wings magically acquired Hriday K. Seraphim flew home for the holidays.

MAGICAL OMELETTES AT KAAKE DA DHABA

Once upon a time there lived a young man called Ritwik in the big city of Delhi. He was a student. A pretty decent one too but he was not extraordinary. In short he was not a world beater but a serious stable steady sort of fellow. A regular guy. There are thousands of them around like him, who are our friends, brothers and other assorted strangers. People who are the backbone of our society and family life. He was one of us.

Like I told you he wasn't extraordinary. Just a face in the crowd but still I feel deep down that he was one of a kind and that his story should be told. Because if it can be told then perhaps his existence wouldn't be meaningless anymore and also because I knew him for a while, when I lived opposite his room in Hakikat Nagar. Both of us are from Patna and we are of the same caste too. We studied at the same school. Ritwik was a couple of years senior to me. Because of all these reasons and some more abstract ones I feel a deep strange kinship with him but the reverse lamentably is not true.

It has now become a compulsion with me to give meaning to his life or rather find meaning in it for myself. So I have decided to tell his story and not let him fade into that vast twilight of lies, conjecture, subterfuge and half baked legends that constitute irredeemable obscurity. I am not a storyteller but I have read some books. I have done English (Hons.) My favourite author is Jeffery Archer. You must have heard of him. My sister loves him too and she should know, after all she is the intellectual of the family. She is working for Zee T.V. Now. Isn't that something?

I will try my best not to botch it all up because there are things that are so weird which happened to him and legends are so many that right now I feel that perhaps mere words will never explain the demented quest that finally did him in. I will spread the thin patchwork quilt of his life before you, dear reader, and you can cull the story out for yourself. People may come up with different versions but according to me this is how it happened.

I will move on now and start from the past. I promise I wont be longwinded and move as fast as I can. All right then like I told you, he was a decent student. In fact he had always topped his class back in the old government school. The principal there had predicted great things for him in the future.

From childhood his father had inculcated in him a dream to join the civil services in general and become an I.A.S officer in particular. Ritwik nursed that dream from childhood through adolescence and early youth. He loved his father and wanted to make him proud but when he failed to clear the mains for two years, desperation set in. Time was running out and also he had no 'reservation'. In a couple of years he would become in D.U. Biharispeak a 'danasur'. A dinosaur. He would be extinct. He knew he could not go back home again. He felt guilty and worthless, always a bad combination for the soul. He knew his whole fraternity, rather our whole fraternity was talking about him in a flippant and trivial manner. He felt bad for his father. He felt like hell inside but he stayed back for one more year. He studied hard working day and night (I stayed in Hakikat Nagar for couple of months at that time) he cleared the P.T. (preliminary test) like always, took the mains in October-November and then waited anxiously for the results. He was under great pressure no doubt. One distant cousin of his had got through to the allied services last year. Ritwik would brood in his room for hours and at night he would wander on the streets of the university. When he would become dogtired he would come back to his room with the green painted walls and sleep the dreamless sleep.

Then one fine day in late march he walked out of his room feeling for the first time in years happy and totally free. He walked towards Kaake da dhaba on the university road for a cup of tea as he had done for months each evening. The dhaba was empty but for couple of blind students from the near-by seva kutir who sat quietly huddled together like pups looking at nothing in particular through their imitation Rayban sunglasses.

Ritwik felt light inside and his mind was clear as water. Accordingly to Kaake he looked just like the Buddha sitting underneath the bodhi tree. Buses, auto-rickshaw and swanky cars sped along on the road towards the university. Ritwik sat there unaffected and outside of it all. He lit a cigarette and felt the cool smoke in his lungs and ordered a special Masala Omelette and a cup of tea. He then closed his eyes. It was the day of salvation for him. After a long long time he felt completely free. The tea came along. It was thick, milky and very sweet and it tasted as rotten as it always did. It was all right. There is stability in conformity. It was hot and he sipped it slowly, savouring it, sucking the thin cream on the top and cupping it with both hands to feel the heat. It was a cool and windy evening.

The blind students started to talk in their naturally loud and belligerent manner with Kaake who was a friend, Philosopher and unwanted guide to all the students who frequented his place. The blind students were very poor and dressed in old and dirty yellowed clothes. They looked unwashed and desperate. Ritwik stared at them with curiosity as if he had discovered them for the first time but in reality they all knew each other well. They were telling Kaake some dirty joke about girls with big boobs and what they would like to do to them. Ritwik didn't hear the end. He had heard it all before. The blind students, loved smutty jokes, he had noticed it before. He felt as if everything was happening around him in a flash back. But whose flash back?

Kaake brought the omelette over in a cracked white plate. It was hot and crisp and spicy. Delicious.

'The Omelette is nice?'

'Very nice' Ritwik answered. He usually enjoyed talking to Kaake but that day it was different. He was sure that Kaake would destroy the exquisite feeling of lightness that he felt.

'I never fry it for long, otherwise it gets all hard and rubbery.'

'It is just perfect. Delicious.' Ritwik said and he knew the next line. He had heard it all before.

'The trick is in selecting the right eggs.'

'Really?'

'The selection is very important.'

'But I thought all eggs were similar. If you have seen one you have seen them all?'

'All eggs are different. They have different personalities and temperament and to make the perfect omelette you have to find the perfect egg unfortunately I myself haven't found it yet'.

'The perfect egg?' Ritwik played along.

'The perfect egg should snuggle in the gap between your fore finger and thumb. It is just one of the criterion. It should fit in totally. Every man has to find his own perfect egg. It varies from person to person.'

'Kaake there is something very important that I must tell you (Kaake nodded eagerly). You are a stupid fool.'

'No, I am a genius and you Ritwik my friend are a stupid fool. One day I am going to find my perfect hen who will lay the perfect eggs and I will serve magical omelettes all around. Soft, crisp and supremely delicious. I will be bigger than Nirulas, K.F.C., McDonalds. Standing room only.'

It was rumoured that 10 years back Kaake had left his hometown in eastern U.P. and boarded the train for the big city to study and prepare for the civil services. Only he wasn't called Kaake then but had a real pan chewing cowbelt name which unfortunately now has been lost in the annals of time. When he failed to clear the preliminary test four times in a row, his father severed all relations and with it all the money. Kaake refused to buckle down under the pressure and he took a loan of 5000/- and set up his small dhaba on the very same spot on the side of university road where he had sat down and shed copious tears each year as a monumental tribute to his shattered dreams. He did a little market research and found that most of the dhaba owners were called 'Kaake' and so … now you know and from there began his quest for the perfect egg and magical omelettes.

'So did you clear it this time?' Kaake asked him after a while.

'What?'

'You know. The mains! The results came out yesterday?' Kaake always made his statement sound like questions.

'Yes, sure, I made it this time.' Ritwik closed his eyes and said slowly.

'What?'

'Yes! Yes! Yes!'

'No!'

'You are an I.A.S. now!'

'If I clear the interview, it depends.'

'You have cleared the mains! No one else before had done it. At least the ones who had my magical omelettes. You are the first. You have broken the Jinx, O pioneer.'

'I must leave now. I have got lots of things linedup.'

'Are you really an I.A.S. now?' The first blind student asked him. He hadn't been listening closely.

'Almost' Ritwik laughed and replied.

'I see.' The second blind student said sottovoce and even he started to laugh.

'I have to run now. I have got so much to do.' Ritwik said that to everyone present and then he started running. Kaake and the blinds cheered him from behind 'Go man go go go' and Ritwik ran and ran and ran. According to my little brother and local legend he never stopped but ran all the way to Patna and stopped only when he reached his home and his father opened the door. Personally I think he took a train, don't you?

Anyway, no one in Delhi ever saw Ritwik again. Kaake tells the story of his magical omelettes and Ritwik to any one who cares to hear. He lives with his illusions and I don't have the heart to break them. He felt hurt that Ritwik had never come to meet him after he became an officer. He told his story to every I.A.S. aspirant who came to his dhaba and they all listened and had his omelettes and evenings there would be standing room only at the place. He is not yet bigger than 'Nirulas' but he is getting there. He has opened one branch in Hudson lines and another one across the road in Outram lines. In Ritwik's honour he called his special omelette 'Ritwik da mayawi Aamlet'. The pre requisite food for all U.P.S.C. candidates. If you don't believe me you can go and take a look. I have never eaten it myself but you can't blame me for that. I am taking the examination myself next year I must admit. I wasn't taking any chances. In this line you can never be too superstitious. Anyway I knew the story. The ones who had it all said, after eating those 'Mayawi' omelettes, that they felt rejuvenated and their withered spirits rose again with each delicious bite.

Meanwhile the day he reached his home Ritwik told his father that he had finally discovered his true calling in life 'About time son' his father said caustically but Ritwik let tha pass and explained to him that his endeavour had to remair ı secret one for now because others were working on it too l ıt he assured his father that when the breakthrough came he would be proud of Ritwik again.

That very night he went out and bought petridishes, slides, dividers, compasses and scales and weights, and of course eggs. His head was full of eggs now. Hen eggs, Duck eggs, turkey eggs, striped eggs, spotted eggs, chipped eggs, eggs of all kinds and hues and he brought them home in brown paper bags and hid them in his book cabinet. Soon he had to throw away all his books and the cabinet became an eggs cabinet. Eggs were all over. They took over his life. From eggs we rise to eggs we sink. He had joined the vast fraternity of egg seekers. He measured them in the morning, then at noon and all through the night. He kept notes of all his findings. He was looking for the mythical perfect egg. The stuff that sweet dreams are made of.

Alas one day his father entered his sanctuary after many months and passed out from the stink.

Finally they put him in the asylum near Ranchi (Ritwik not his father), but even there he has smuggled in his calipers. He still looks for ways to further his vast knowledge on eggs. He hasn't given up. His condition has been described as being one of acute compulsive eggomania. He has also written a thesis based upon his findings and sent it to M.I.T. (Massachusetts not Muzaffarpur). I know that because I sent it myself. He gave it to me when I went to meet him couple of months back. It was the least I could do for him.

Ward 22 and you will be taken to a nice young man with luminous eyes who would after some time ask you cordially if you could by any chance provide him with some eggs for an experiment he is conducting for the welfare of all mankind. 'Just one truck load will do'.

OUTLAWS

It was a cool sunny December afternoon and all over Patna the winter holidays had just begun. The schools were closed. It was a happy and cheerful time for Ritwik and Subir. They lived in the old Bengali colony of Kadam Kuan and had been friends since childhood. Before them their elder brothers had been friends and in a way they were continuing a tradition. Both of them were Bengalies, both of them were fair and wore their hair long, but Subir was taller and thinner; somewhat a dandy, Ritwik the more serious of the two, slower of the two. There was a slight similarity in their appearance – people often mistook them to be brothers. They had done everything together; learned to play cricket together, to ride the bike, whistle at the girls, listen to the same kind of music, been in the same fights, and to top it all, had fallen in love with the same girls and that too many a time. They had grown up together fighting, laughing, sharing, on the same streets of Kadam Kuan.

They spent their days playing cricket in the mornings and in the evenings they looked at the girls in the market place and smoked as many cigarettes as they could. They had no worries and no fear. They were as free as birds. If they had wings they would have flown to the sun, surely. Those were the golden days of their friendship and adolescence.

So one cool sunny December afternoon they walked to the small cigarette shop at the corner, bought two cigarettes and lit up. The cigarette shop was situated at the gate of a large mansion. Nobody except an old Bengali widow lived there. The whole thing was slowly crumbling down, more and more cracks appeared on the faded walls each year, worn and weary with age and loneliness – but it stood there inspite of it all. Both Subir and Ritwik could remember the time when it used to be so beautiful and they would play in the vast courtyard inside. There used to be a guava tree inside the courtyard but it was chopped down long time ago. One of their earliest childhood friends used to live there. They had left for Calcutta eight years back. Bengalies were slowly leaving the place. Everybody was going away. Only the old remained in the beautiful old mansions. The young had moved away and soon the old would die and the houses sold off but still the Bengali flavour remained in the air. During Durga puja they still put up the best puja pandal in town. The money wasn't there like before but the heart stayed generous and proud. The cigarette and paan shop was an encroachment.

They pulled low their baseball caps over their eyes and watched out for relatives and other assorted senior citizens. They didn't want to be caught smoking. It would be a big scandal if they were caught – after all they came from such respectable families. They talked about some of the neighbourhood girls and decided they were all stuckup bitches, not much worth talking about anyway.

After some time Subir asked the shopkeeper for some ball point refills which he knew the man kept at the back the shop. As the man turned around Subir took a packet of Gold Flakes from the front rack and slipped it into his pocket.

He looked at the refills but then decided that he didn't need them any more and both of them walked away from the shop.

'Why did you do that?' Ritwik said to him in Bengali, his eyes burning with excitement.

'Why? Because I wanted to have them.'

'But it isn't right, is it?'

'I don't know about that but you do want to smoke, don't you?'

'Yes.'

'And you don't have any money?'

'No' Ritwik shook his head, realising he had already lost

the argument.

'See, now the problem is solved, we don't have to buy any more cigarettes today. we have saved 20 rupees. We can watch a movie tonight at Regent.'

'But, Subir, it is stealing, we shouldn't steal!'

'All right it is stealing but so what? Nothing matters.'

'Is it the first time or ...'

'Remember all those Gold Flakes that you smoked yesterday, trying to impress the girls, yes? Well those were free too.'

'But it doesn't feel right you know. We are not thieves.'

'You are right, we are not thieves. We are uh ..., well we are, how shall I put it, all right ...., well we are just outlaws, yes, that's right, we are just a couple of cool outlaws. Don't you feel the thrill of it? Kind of like Robin Hood.'

'Robin Hood stole from the rich to give to the poor. But we are going to smoke it ourselves, won't we dear Subir.'

'All right, we may not be Robin Hoods but we are still outlaws'.

'We could have been caught and then everybody would have known, everybody ...'

'Who gives a fuck and anyway we didn't get caught.' Subir crushed the butt and smiled beatifically at Ritwik.

They walked in silence for sometime, the thrill of their adventure still clinging to their walk, making Subir swagger and Ritwik slouch. They looked at the girls in the market place from the corner of their eyes. They were happy and at peace with everything.

They didn't want anything else. It was Subir's birthday the next day, so, after a while Ritwik asked him about it, just to break the silence and start a conversation again.

'It is your birthday tomorrow, isn't it?'

'Yes, I am bored with birthdays. It makes me feel old and grey. I am too old for birthdays. I want to fuck some girls now.'

'Even old people have birthdays. You can't escape the birthdays, only when you die, there can't be any more birthdays.' Ritwik said to him in a patronising manner.

'You know Ritwik, you make me sick. You are a bloody poet, you read too many books. You make me sick, I am positive, you make me sick.'

'And you make me sick, you thief.'

'I am not a thief, I told you. I am an outlaw. I am a 16 year-old outlaw. Don't you remember what Bob Dylan said?' Subir asked Ritwik indignantly.

'Sure. To live outside the law you have to be honest.'

'Yes, that's right.' Subir agreed and smiled and fished out a cigarette and lit it with as much coolness as he could manage.

'But you know what Subir, it doesn't mean a thing, what Dylan said – stealing is still stealing.'

'Now, you know more than Dylan!'

'If you look at it rationally, it doesn't mean a thing. It's just stylish American Crap.' Ritwik knew how much Subir loved Dylan and regretted saying it the moment he uttered it, Subir didn't seem to mind but he became more serious.

'You have to be honest, I am honest. I took just what I needed, I could have taken two or may be three packs but I took just one I am honest.' Subir said it slowly. He knew in his heart he was right.

'Don't do it again, all right. I am telling you.'

'I don't have to listen to you Ritwik.'

'Don't ever steal anything, all right?'

'You call yourself a bloody poet and you don't have any understanding of life. When there is no thrill there can't be any poetry, no life. It is the thrill that is important above all things in life.' Subir pushed back his cap, put his fingers into his hair and pushed it back, narrowed his eyes and then pulled low his cap again.

'We don't have to steal, its something very low and degrading, even if its thrilling I won't ever do it myself.' Ritwik went on and on like a stuck record.

'Then don't.'

'But you will steal like some common thief.' Ritwik said to him in mock anger and took out a cigarette from the pack.

'I don't want to be respectable, may be you do, but I really don't give a fuck what anybody thinks, what you think. And I'm not a fucking thief. Don't you ever call me that again.'

'If you promise not to do that again, I won't', Ritwik said to him seriously.

'Alright, alright, I won't. Happy now?'

'Sure.'

So they walked silently, together, each one happy in the company of the other. Life was beautiful, magical and flowing smoothly and to them their friendship was the greatest gift of all. They didn't realise it fully but they could sense it. There was Rock Music and Cricket and beautiful girls to make love to if only they could get the chance, but for now they were content to just talk over the phone late into the night. It was a wonderful life. Nothing ever could go wrong.

'Did you see that girl?' Subir nudged Ritwik and asked him.

'The one in the red salwar suit, right?' Ritwik said looking at the girl in question who was crossing the street just ahead of them. She was an exceptionally beautiful girl with long auburn hair parted in the middle, with a small pointed nose, red, red lips just meant for kissing, small tight breasts that shook slightly as she walked. She was older and obviously rich; both Ritwik and Subir were smitten.

'Let's follow her' Subir suggested and Ritwik accepted as always. Subir was the leader, Ritwik was the poet. They followed her into a music shop and Ritwik said to Subir, 'She ooks old, must be over 20.' 'Yes, nice isn't she?'

'Nice'

The girl cool and oblivious to the turmoil she had caused sauntered into the shop and flitted from shelf to shelf, touching a tape here, a tape there, reading the contents, smiling to herself, pushing back her hair with her long fingers, her eyes effulgent and expectant, totally ignoring the boys who walked a step behind trying to look serious and sophisticated. Just then a man entered – tall and with a face that could only be called pretty, with long eye lashes and greenish grey eyes, red thin lips like a slash and a long fragile jaw with a dimple wedged in the right cheek. He went up to the girl and gently tapped her shoulders as if she were a window pane and her face lit up with a spreading smile. They walked out together.

The boys watched her go out and they felt crushed and defeated. She was so pretty. She had taken out with her the 'Something special' that was in the air, a hope, a romance, a story, an adventure, thrill …

'Bitch but nice bitch' Subir said mournfully!

'Nice wonderful sexy sexy bitch' Ritwik agreed.

Suddenly the adventure had ended and there was nothing more to do. They looked at the music tapes. Rock music was their shared passion. They read anything they could find on the subject and listened to whatever tapes they could get. They didn't have the luxury of discrimination. From the floor to the false ceiling thousands of music tapes were stacked on the glass shelves and the reflected light from those caught their eyes. They looked at the tapes and wished that they were rich. They wished they had 100 rupees.

'They have Dylan's *Blood on the Tracks* album, can you believe it.'

'This is a fucking classic. A real classic' Subir laughed and looked at the tape wistfully, read the contents again, shook his head and finally put back the tape in its proper place on the shelf. He then ambled over to the other side where the Books and Magazine section was but Ritwik didn't move from that place, his hands inside his jacket were clenched into fists and he continued looking at the wonderful glossy tapes and wished again that he were rich.

After sometime they walked out of the shop. They were both a bit subdued now. They walked back towards their homes, back to the familiar streets; the earlier spring missing from their walk. Subir was graver, as if he had learnt something profound and unavoidable back in the shop. Then he thought about the girl and he fell light, glad inside. Both of them would never forget that beautiful girl all their lives. She would always be there. She had meant different things to both Ritwik and Subir. She had promised different things to both of them. Subir just wanted to reach home early now and lie down, watch T.V. or masturbate maybe, and in the evening they would go to Regent where they were showing a revival of *Sholay*. Things would be better in the evening.

'Subir I am sorry I was angry at you earlier.' Ritwik said

after a while.

'It is all right.' Saying sorry and acknowledging it were always a tortuous job and the important thing was to get it over with as quickly as possible.

'You know, you were right about the thrill part and about life and poetry, it is pretty important I guess, you have to be free. 'What's life without a little passion.' Ritwik repeated their favourite catch phrase from a popular motor cycle ad.

'Yes,' Subir laughed and repeated the phrase.

'And one thing more Subir ...'

'What?'

'Happy Birthday' Ritwik said to him and thrust into his hands the Bob Dylan tape he had coveted so much. *Blood on the Tracks.*

'You didn't!' Subir stared at the tape incredulously.

'Yes I did.' Ritwik said and embraced him. They both laughed and their laughter so wild and free merged into the shared laughter of many such golden friendships that were forged on small trivial moments such as this and their laughter would never die and nor would that moment, perhaps later sadness would make its inroads and life would create fissures but for now all that could wait.

THE WOMEN

If you went straight down a certain avenue and then turned right and again after a while left you would enter one of the oldest localities in Patna and like most old places you would find it to be extremely contradictory in nature, Professors, Doctors, I.A.S. Officers, Civil Servants and other white collar representatives were there but also with them lived the pimps, the petty thieves, the small time extortionists, poets, revolutionaries of diverse faith, shopkeepers and in the words of Faulkner 'all breeding and spawning together'. The upper class people high on culture, low on cash lived in old delapidated mansions with a portico and a courtyard inside with a guava tree in it and a mango tree in the backyard and the others lived in peculiar drab brown buildings which seemed to have mushroomed overnight and which were made to occupy as little space as possible in terms of width. These buildings had small rooms like cells with a little window on the side for ventilation and were unavoidably hot and stuffy at most times of the year.

In one of these rooms a man sat crosslegged on the floor brooding. A thick yellow candle burned at the end of the room and he watched the flicker of the flames and the play of shadows his wife made as she sat making the evening meal for him. For hours the electricity was cut off in the area.

In the past one year so much had changed. The rooms appeared as if they had shrunk in his absence and the very streets had become narrower. He felt like a stranger in his own home. It was from this very place he had left for the countryside as ordered a year back. He hoped to God that nobody had seen him enter the house. They were still looking for him, he knew that. They never gave up. He knew it was a mistake but things were getting unbearable. Maybe he was getting too soft. He still believed in the 'struggle' but his heart was not in it anymore. He had to see his wife and son. His wife had sounded desperate, almost hysterical in her last letter. 'It could be a trap. Do not leave, you know we can't trust anyone,' the area commander had said to him but for once he had defied the orders. He had to see her once, sometimes even the fact that he was married seemed unreal to him and only when her letters would arrive months after they were written, the piercing reality, the hopelessness of their situation would strike home and he would become deluged with guilt. He shouldn't have married and sometimes he wished that he hadn't. It was a mess.

His son was almost five years old and was very shy and had refused to come near him. The boy had totally forgotten his father and the dim mythic image of his 'real' father locked in his memory refused to come to terms with this tangible reality. His son was sleeping now and he would be out of the house before dawn. He wondered if it would ever end.

'I can't stay the whole night. I'll be out before dawn,' he said to his wife in a whisper. It had almost become second nature for him to whisper nowadays.

She looked at him. The months of living like a fugitive had taken its toll on her husband's once handsome frame. He had lost weight and his long lustrous hair was cropped short and had become thinner over the top. She could see the whiteness of the scalp through the short bristles. Somehow that made her feel vaguely disturbed. He had shaved off his beard and didn't quite look like the man she had once loved anymore. He has grown so quiet, she thought. Two hours had passed since he had arrived but still she felt as if she were in the room with a total stranger. She went and opened the window and peered out into the darkness. She felt a vague sense of fear as if this long cherished for intimacy could be snuffed out at any moment.

'Can't you stay a day or two?' She asked him timidly, knowing all the time what his answer would be.

'I wish I could but it is too much of a risk,' he said quietly.

All the time that he was underground, moving about at nights through the villages and moffusil towns of South and Central Bihar holding meetings in the middle of the fields in the dead of night and training the cadre to shoot and make bombs near the river edges, writing pamphlets that endorsed the 'partyline,' the struggle that had changed from 'class' to 'caste' in ground reality and whose very ideology he himself wasn't sure about anymore but he wrote them nevertheless, living rough like a fugitive his only wish had been to spend sometime with his family but now when he was with them he couldn't wait to move out again. Fear had suffussed through every pore of his body and coursed down his bloodstream. He had to run again. He knew that. He felt as if he had never known her and the life they had lived earlier had perhaps happened to a different couple altogether but at the same time he wanted to stay with her, make love to her slowly like she loved, explore again the familiar comfort of her body and somehow tear down the unseen wall of silence that lay like a dead child between them.

'I hope you get the money they send,' he asked her after a while. 'Yes. They are very particular. Money is not a problem. There is more than we need. I was thinking of putting him in a school now,' she said to him. 'He is still so small.' The man replied.

'He is old enough. All the other boys of his age are in schools.'

'Do whatever you think is best?'

'You have become so thin, don't you take your meals regularly?'

'I eat whenever I can, like the rest of them. It is just that I don't seem to put on weight anymore. It is better this way, less of me to carry around.' He smiled at her for the first time.

'Have you got a woman to look after you over there.'

'I don't stay at one place for long.'

'You must have had women to care for you sometimes,' she asked once more. 'They were not important. I don't even remember their faces.' She put his dinner in front of him and he ate in silence.

'When will you come again!' She asked staring longingly at his face.

'I don't know. Patna is too dangerous for me. Maybe I'll call you over to some place safe if I find it.' As he said this he knew it would never happen that way ever.

'Can't you take me with you? We could leave right now,' she said in a voice that had suddenly become quite hysterical. 'And what about our son?' He asked taken aback a bit.

'The neighbours can take care of him for the time being. I just want to be with you. I can't bear the loneliness anymore. I can't make sacrifices anymore. Everyday I get nightmares. I think about you constantly. I have seen you dead many times. I can't sleep anymore. I keep the lights on the whole night.' She was on the verge of tears and her face twisted with pain and sadness but in that sadness there was also hope for the future. Hope that he would say yes.

'You can't come with me. You know the party work. You wouldn't be safe ever. I can't take you and you must take care of our son because I can't.' They were silent for sometime and then she said slowly, 'Have you ever taken anyone's life?'

'Why do you ask that?'

'I just want to know. I must know.'

He didn't say anything for a while and then he looked at her thoughtfully and said. 'No, I haven't but I have taught others to kill so I guess it is the same thing. I have seen terrible things. I was there. I have been a witness.' She could see the truth of the statement stamped on his face.

'Do you think all this is worth it?'

'Killings are never worth anything, they can't ever be part of any long term solution. I know that but it is not as simple as that. One must fight for one's dignity, for the simple right to live as humans and in this our caste haunted land, there is no dignity without protest. So I protest. But there are times when I do feel that somewhere something has gone horribly wrong and rather than rectify it we have messed it up some more. I am just a very small cog in a large wheel, perhaps the people at the high command have the larger picture in their mind. I hope they are sure about what they are doing but then they are hardly ever in the field. There are times when I feel that I am doing something worthwhile, when I raise a sub-human dalit to human existence, give him some pride, teach him his rights, I feel calm then. There are too many things involved now. It is not a matter of ideology anymore. It's not simple at all. Let us leave the judgement to history. Terrible things have been done to us and in return we have done the same. It will go on. But it is true I am getting tired. My heart is not in it anymore. Once I believed passionately in our cause. I am not so sure now. In my mind I have too many questions and not enough answers. So I do not know if all this is worth it or not but I know that I will go on doing it because once when I was very young it had given me a cause, something to believe in and it is very important for a man to believe in something, have faith in something external to him. I haven't talked this much in weeks!' He finished out of breath.

'Why don't you give it all up! It would have been better if you were in jail, look at Kashyap. You could do the same. I could visit you then. May be they will pardon you like Kashyap. You would be safe. We could be together.'

'You don't understand, do you! He was an informer and I can't ever be that. He won't live for long on the outside. You know what they do to informers, don't you! You will starve, you stupid women. Bring the candle over here!'

She brought the candle closer and his face gleamed in the light. There were dark circles beneath his eyes and his fair skin had darkened as if something had burnt him from the inside. She touched his fear denuded face, running her fingers over his lips, his sunken eyes. He stopped eating and looked up to her with surprise and tenderness.

He pulled her toward himself and kissed her softly on the lips. She pulled him down on top of her and they made love. Afterwards as she lay beside him he felt an uncontrollable urge to cry, he felt a terrible emptiness. Like a bone with the marrow all sucked dry. Just then there was heavy banging on the door.

'It's the police!' He said simply while reaching for his pistol.

'Don't. They won't hurt you.' She said to him hysterically. He looked at her and he knew everything.

They broke the door. He put the pistol down. His son was sleeping in the other room. He didn't want to wake him up. He wanted everything to be done quietly. There was no point in fighting anymore.

'You fool, you stupid fool!' He said to her once but in an undertone so low that it looked as if he were talking to himself. Maybe he was.

The City S.P. with two inspectors and ten constables entered the room. The S.P. was in plain clothes. He felt a curious sense of pride as he counted the number of policemen sent out to capture him. They didn't put handcuffs on him and he was a little surprised. They just grabbed him and pushed him out of capture him. They didn't put handcuffs on him and he was a little surprised. They just grabbed him and pushed him out of the room, he looked at his wife, tears streaming down her face, and he wondered what for! He felt a kind of peace as if suddenly everything had been decided for him. There was no choice anymore.

As he stepped into the street he could feel the stillness of the night. No one was on the streets but he could feel their eyes on him from shadowy rooms and darkened balconies peering out at him, staring at him. He was tired. Someone grabbed his arms from behind. He was too surprised to react but it had been at the back of his mind. They hadn't put handcuffs on him. He was hit on the side of his face with a rifle butt and he fell down, hit his face on the street and broke his nose. They shot him twice keeping their rifles just inches away from his body. A silent scream rose in her throat. She was still at the doorstep. She tried to scream but could only mumble incoherently, then she fainted.

She filed a case against the City S.P. but nothing came out of it. There were no witnesses they said, there was never any witness but then it was expected. In a curious quirk of fate the S.P. was gunned down near Jamshedpur while he was returning home with his wife from a party late at night, couple of years later.

Everything was forgotten after a while but even after the headlines die, the women live on. They could never forget the way his body would jerk up with each shot like some big fish that still thrashes around after being clubbed on the shore. They would remember that for the rest of their lives. All through the night, they still keep the lights on.

THE ADOLESCENTS

'Can you please call her, it's room A7, I think.'

He said to the girl who was going inside the hostel.

'Sure. A7?'

'Yes A7, Mira Verma. Thank you.' He called out after her and then turned back towards the hostel gate. He heard her call out Mira's name, 'Mira Verma, A7 visitor'. He waited down by the gate under the shade of the bougainvillea creepers and the diffused November sun filtered through the pink flowers and made patterns by his feet. In the small covered portico, which was called the 'Cage' Coca Cola-Pepsi a small black mongrel pup whom the girls had adopted played with flowers. He was the guard dog.

The sunlight felt warm on the heavy flannel shirt that he

wore and he felt strangely happy. It was one of those rare moments that are nostalgia before they are over.

He closed his eyes and turned his face towards the sun and he realised that if he didn't control his impulses he would start smiling – he felt that happy.

'Ritwik, when did you return?' Someone asked him in Bengali and he opened his eyes.

'Today in the afternoon.' He answered in Bengali and smiled his most charming smile which he reserved for girls like her. She was a friend all right.

'Nobody informed me that you were here, in the hostel I mean.'

She said again in Bengali. She had for some time lived in Bengal and had picked up the rudiments of the language, just the basics, and she had the strange notion, which many non-bengalies have that if they pronounced every 'a' like an 'o' the Hindi they speak would magically turn into Bengali. Maybe he was supposed to feel flattered, Ritwik thought.

'I am waiting for Mira.' He informed her in Hindi.

'Mira?, Oh I thought … never mind. Shall I call her?'

She switched over to English and he felt grateful.

'No, No, it is alright, I have already asked one of the girls to inform her.'

'So how are things going now – studies and all?'

'I am coasting along, nothing new.' He answered and looked

at his watch.

'You know what, you remind me of Uttam Kumar.'

Last time it was some other movie actor, Ritwik could not recall the name.

'I don't like Uttam Kumar.' He felt the necessity to lie and then hated himself but it was all right. It was required.

'You don't? Are Bengalies not supposed to adore him or something?'

'Are they?' He asked softly. He wished she would go away.

He looked at his watch again.

She smiled and said 'I have got so much work to do, the college festivals are coming along, I am doing the choreography this year.'

'That's great, you must be very busy.' He give her the cue.

'Yes, I have to run, bye. I will be seeing you some other time.' She said and walked out of the gate. Ritwik watched her for sometime, lit a cigarette and upturned his face to the sun again. It was already 5 minutes since the girl had gone inside.

After a while Mira's roommate came out. She was from a small town in Bihar, she had a strange slow old woman's gait. She was doing an honours course in Psychology.

'She has gone to Kamla Nagar.' She said to him. She knew about him but he had a feeling that she didn't much approve of him.

'Has she gone alone?'

'No, with some friends.'

'Do you know when she will be back?'

'In an hour or so. Did she know that you were coming?'

'I don't know, I don't think so.'

'I will inform her that you had come.'

'No that is all right. I think I will wait.'

She looked at him for a second longer than was necessary and then slowly turned towards the cage, where the phone was. 'Thank you.' He called loudly after her, and went out of the gate, walked towards the Ice Cream seller and sat down on the brown sack cloth that was spread on the pavement. He could watch the street and the hostel gate from there. It was nice to be back. The one month in Patna had been nice too but now he was glad to be back. Delhi was beautiful in November and he wanted to get on with his life.

When you want something to happen it never happens quickly because you are always thinking about it, and when you are waiting for something time moves as if on crutches. Ritwik promised himself that he won't think about it. He was happy sitting there, he knew Mira would be there and he didn't glance at his watch all the time that he was waiting for her.

After an hour or so, he saw a rickshaw with three girls, one fat, one medium, one lean perched precariously upon it, coming fast, down Chhatra Marg. The lean one was Mira. The rickshaw stopped in front of him and he crushed his cigarette under his foot and smiled.

Mira was smiling too but she was conscious of her friends; they were looking at him from underneath their averted eyes. They had suddenly become very business-like and serious. They had been laughing in the rickshaw, their hair blowing in the wind. He had seen that.

Mira came towards him smiling and wishing in her heart that she had worn something else other than the dirty black jeans. She had wanted to wash it on Sunday but had overslept.

'I've been waiting for a long time.'

'I'm sorry. I never thought …'

'But you knew I was coming back today, didn't you?'

'Yes, I got the news but I thought maybe you would come tomorrow or the day after, sometime later anyway.'

'I had to see you today.'

She was silent for a while and then he suggested 'Let's walk.'

'Yes, let's go over to the University garden, the flowers are in full bloom now. I am glad that you are back.'

'And it is nice to know that you are glad that I am back.'

He laughed and she looked into his eyes and saw that he wasn't lying. They walked towards the University Co-operative Store, by the side of Meghdoot Hostel, up the incline of heaped up soil, into the green clearing where some kids were practising Kung Fu. They have built big cement steps over there now.

'Why didn't you write to me?' Ritwik looked at her sideways and asked.

'I didn't have your address.'

'You could have easily got it.'

'Yes, I don't know, I was not sure, were you expecting a letter?'

'I thought you might write, you always said that you loved to write letters, I hoped maybe you will add one more to the list.'

'Even you didn't write to me.'

'No. I wanted to. But I didn't know where to begin, what to say, all that, but I did want to. I had your address.'

'You never say anything clearly.'

'I am moody and stupid but you know that don't you?'

'I don't know much about you but I like you, I feel comfortable with you, I think I have told you that. I am not eloquent at all.'

'Did you write anything in the autumn break?'

'Yes, two short stories, both of them are of my childhood – very simple stories really, I will read it out to you sometime.'

'You should have brought them today.'

'I don't know. I have to work on them somemore. They are not very good but they are honest, I will read them out to you. When I was writing them I thought about reading them out to you.'

Some students were playing Volleyball down by the side of the University garden. Some of them turned and looked at Ritwik and Mira as they passed and whistled. Mira giggled, looked at Ritwik, he smiled too.

They sat down on a wide cement bench and looked at some kids playing tag on the grass, after a while a small dog ambled over and joined the games.

The sun had gone down and lights come on and the whole garden was bathed in a glaring bright orange light. Couples moved among the trees and the pathways with arms around each other's waists. Mira and Ritwik oblivious to the world talked away. They talked about many things, the films they had seen, the books that they had read, how really awful *Hum Aapke Hain Kaun* was, the crazy new Hindi film-songs, about Arvind Swamy and Manisha Koirala, about their families, common friends and finally about death, suicide, poetry of Dylan Thomas and Guru Dutt, but never once did they discuss anything that was remotely personal as if the subject were too painful to both of them. They didn't talk about the thing that both of them so much wanted to talk about. It was already being discussed in the hostel. They knew that. Ritwik could sense a kind of darkness hovering about and he was confused. There were so many things that had no answers.

'What do you friends think about me?'

'Does it matter to you?' she asked him softly.

'Yes if it matters to you.' He said to her in Bengali.

'What did you say?'

He repeated what he had said in English.

'No, it doesn't.' she looked at him defiantly.

They were silent again for sometime and Ritwik lit another cigarette.

'And what do your friends think?' She asked him.

'They think you are a bit dark.' He laughed.

'A bit dark?' It was her turn to laugh.

'Okay, dark.' He accepted.

Two constables strolled over the pathway and walked past them, then one of them noticed the couple and sauntered over to them. 'What are you two doing here?' He asked in a heavily accented Punjabi Hindi.

'We are sitting here, talking.' Ritwik pointed it out to them.

'You can't sit here, go away.'

'It is the University garden, anyone can sit here and we are students.'

'What are you two doing here then, after dark, studying?'

They chuckled among themselves and one of them spat on the grass.

Mira whispered to him 'Let's go, it is time anyway.'

He felt his eyes burning within but he didn't say anything and he didn't get up.

'Show me your identity card.' The constable who had spat on the grass said to Ritwik.

'I haven't got it here with me.'

But Mira had taken her card out and they peered at it like the illiterates they were, for sometime, and then gave it back to her.

'Alright, but we know all about you 'students', what goes on here.' And they chuckled again and continued on their beat.

'I feel so … I feel so … defiled.' Mira whispered to him but he wasn't listening to her anymore.

'Let's go.' He said after a while.

'We can sit here for sometime now.' She said wryly to him.

'Let's get out of here. I am sorry I brought you here.'

'Ritwik, it was my idea and this is nothing new.'

'But they had no right, fucking common constables.'

'Don't get angry now.'

'I shouldn't have brought you here.' They walked towards the hostel slowly. Ritwik felt the warm happiness that he had felt in the evening drain out of him and now only the sharp chill remained. They walked through the trees, the path ahead of them lay dark and bare.

He looked at her – her sadness and loneliness complimented his with her warm and slightly bemused stare. She was confused too.

He slid one arm around her shoulders and pulled her unto himself and kissed her on her right cheek. She tasted of summer rain and mangoes.

'Why did you do that?'

She wasn't hurt but the question mark was there in her eyes.

'I don't know, just felt like it.'

'You are very bold.'

'I am very afraid, I am not bold at all. There are many things that I don't understand.'

She didn't say anything but walked silently by his side, his arm was off her shoulder now. It was getting chilly as the temperature dipped and cold wind ripped through the trees. 'I won't come tomorrow.' The sadness that he felt wasn't like anything he had felt before and she remained silent and brooding. Slowly they walked down the incline by the side of Meghdoot hostel, some P.G. students were sitting around smoking and talking.

Mira thought about the empty gossip, the lukewarm evening tea and the soggy pastries, the new dress that she had worn just once, the poems that had remained unwritten, dreams that had become brittle as old pressed flowers between the covers of her heart and said 'I want you to come tomorrow. I want this. Let's not rush into anything but let's do this, after all "Tomorrow is another day." She looked at him, there were tears in her eyes.

'I will wear my brown turtle neck tomorrow.' He hugged his arms and said. He felt nice and happy all over again.

They had reached the hostel gate and some of her friends

were staring at them.

'They are staring at us.' She whispered to him.

'Frankly my dear, I don't give a fuck.'

She laughed and hoped that nobody had heard him.

'I will see you tomorrow Bye.' She turned back and went inside the hostel.

'I will come at 3 o'clock, just be outside.' He shouted after her, making sure everybody heard him, especially her friends, then he lit a cigarette, shivered and blew at his fingers, rubbed his palms and started walking up the street rapidly striding. He would definitely wear the brown turtle neck tomorrow, he promised himself.

A SCENE FROM CLASS STRUGGLE IN PATNA

We were coming back from the film society screening of *The Tin Drum.* It was after 10 p.m. and the streets were mostly deserted. Patna goes to sleep early in the winters.

Anupam was driving the scooter. He is couple of years elder to me and was then working as a cultural correspondent of a leading Patna daily. I, on the other hand, had just completed my intermediate in science, and was waiting to leave for Delhi. I was 18 years old and had no plans for the future whatsoever. Come to think of it, even almost a decade later nothing much has changed. I had some vague notion of making movies one day but all that was in the future and the very thought even at that time seemed a trifle absurd to me. I loved the movies. There were no two ways about it. I was obsessed with them. At that particular time of my adolescence, I thought I knew more about movies than anybody else in the world. I knew almost everything, all the trivia, but it was a hollow book based knowledge, good for quiz shows and impressing the girls. But it was fun and it required enormous scholarship and remember it was the time before the satellite revolution and Star Movies and HBO and TCM and all the other movie channels, which have made movie buffs out of everybody in India. At the film society that month it was the 'German Directors' Retrospective. We had started on friday evening with the excellent Wim Wenders movie *Alice in the City* which like all other Wenders movies of the seventies had a terrific rock-n-roll score. On saturday we watched Klaus Kinski hamming it up as *Fitzcarraldo* in Werner Herzog's obsessive movie about an Irish man who wanted to bring Caruso to the Amazon. Later on when I watched *Burden of Dreams,* Les Blank's landmark documentary on the making of *Fitzcarraldo* in Delhi I realised how obsessive and self-indulgent 'Art' can become. That and *Hearts of Darkness* are a window to the soul of film-making which I recommend to anyone who are even half in love with the magic that is cinema.

I remember I couldn't sleep that night after watching *Fitzcarraldo*. Something about that Irishman had disturbed me, his manic single mindedness, almost psychotic persistence and obsessive behaviour, in which I had perhaps seen a reflection of myself. Maybe even old Fitz was just an overgrown adolescent. You can't be that obsessive and not retain part of your adolescence in some measure. Obsession and adolescence go hand in hand. Everywhere.

I can recall only two more movies which affected me that way: one was Ray's *Apur Sansar* which is still to me the greatest love-story ever made and the other was Scorsese's *Taxi Driver,* which, perhaps, has the most perfect screenplay ever for a Hollywood movie. I must have seen both of those movies over 20 times and could at that time give a shot by shot division narration of both at a moment's notice for any poor fool who happened to be nearby. More often than not it was Anupam who incidentally had absolutely hated *Taxi Driver* and whom I was zealously trying to convert.

And so on sunday evening it was Volkar Schlondorff's 1979 winner for the best film oscar *The Tin Drum* about which we had already heard that it had lots of nudity. So one had waited with extreme excitement. I tried reading the Gunther Grass Novel when I was 15 but had found it to be too dense and couldn't ever finish reading it though of course I gave the impression to the contrary to everybody else present that day for the show. Now that Grass has won the Nobel Prize for literature, maybe I should take it out of the carton, dust the silver fish off and put it back on my desk for all and sundry to see and have a sudden debilitating attack of inferiority complex. Nothing like an unread laureate novel for decimating humbug in one's friends. Works like poison. Everytime.

The movie didn't disappoint. After the show there were a

lot of red-faced middle class housewives whose carnal knowledge if not their minds must have expanded exponentially that night. Anupam and I could barely suppress our laughter. We both had thoroughly enjoyed the movie and images from it would cling to our memory all our lives. The voluminous skirt of Osker's grand-mother under which a man found his salvation, the single pussy hair stuck on young Osker's tongue after a bout of honey prospecting, his terrible hypnotic stare and drum playing, his growth stunted while Nazism grew, his mother weeping in the bedroom, being diddled by his uncle (his real father?) while the father sits reading the newspaper in the next room, the dead flyblown squid (or was it a fish?) on the beach....

Afterwards we went to a café nearby and had couple of kathi rolls and discussed the movie. Rather we deconstructed it. At night Anupam would write about them for his regular column. We talked about the camera angles and the magic realist treatment, the colour schemes and all the intellectual claptrap. We were like Truffaut and Godard in the *Cahiers-du-Cinema* office. Thinking about those days brings a wry smile to my cynical face. Those were good days. Naïve, idyllic, carefree days.

Then something happened. An incident. A minor one in retrospect. But one which both of us haven't forgotten to this day; it is a topic to which we still invariably get round to after half a bottle of Old Monk. Well, we almost got lynched.

The Mandal Commission agitation was still going on at that time. The whole of our country stood divided like never before. And Bihar, my precious caste-ridden republic never actually recovered from that blow. Now one was either a 'forward' or a 'backward' and being either in a wrong place at the right time could land one in serious trouble.

Patna was relatively quiet except for a few random bandhs and police firings but it was from the countryside, the villages, the smaller towns, that one heard the real horror stories. Things which started then have continued to this day. The hierarchy collapsed to some extent but beneath the ashes of the old time feudalism, ambers still smouldered. It took on a different shape and continued anew. The characters changed but essentially the play remained the same. Earlier that year, Laloo Yadav on a pro-poor and anti upper caste mandate had ridden into town and had already made Patna the clown's paradise, which it would remain for years to come.

There were still one or two demonstrations a week. The university was closed. I, on the other hand was unaffected by all this because at that time I was totally apolitical, though sometimes fancied myself as being on the 'left'. Why? Well, because Ché was left and so was Godard and Rocha and Saeed Mirza and because Marxists were an anathema to my posh upper class society. I was like Jimmy Dean. A rebel without a pause.

We entered Nala road, laughing and talking loudly against the wind, and in no hurry to reach our homes. Anupam was driving very slowly. Suddenly there appeared on the road a drunken man on a bicycle. He tottered comically before hitting the scooter, lost his balance, fell and passed out on the street. A look of profound satisfaction spread on his florid face.

We too lost our balance and fell. Afterwards I crouched near the man and said to Anupam 'He is all right. Totally drunk but unhurt.'

'Leave him. He will be all right. Let us move out quickly.' Anupam's voice, usually a firm baritone, had slipped down an octave or two. Then I saw the reason. Half a dozen men had gathered from the footpath, where they had perhaps been sleeping and were now moving towards us. There were others who were watching from the dark, they would join in when the fun really began. All of them had half their faces covered with shawls. Most of them were labourers who worked as servants on daily wages in our homes or nearby construction sites.

A roar of 'Maar daala, maar daala' went up and within seconds we were surrounded. One of the men, a reed thin wiry chap tried to snatch the keys but I caught hold of his hand and told him that it wasn't our fault that the mishap happened; moreover the cyclist was very inebriated. Also he wasn't hurt or anything but to no avail. The mob refused to listen to reason.

As I now think about that night, another more recent night comes to mind when a group of kids from well-heeled families ran over couple of street dwellers in a B.M.W. in Delhi but eventually nothing much happened to them. They went scot-free. A decade back, were we any different from these clean cut kids who crushed to death several human beings, dragging one of them for a length of time entangled in the wheels but refusing to stop? Perhaps we wouldn't have been so cruel. So callous. But we too wouldn't have stopped if we hadn't lost our balance.

No one stops in Patna after an accident. One is taught never to do so. No one actually says it in so many words but it is there in the atmosphere and one inculcates it just by breathing.

They were in no mood to listen. They just wanted to lynch these affluent good looking high caste kids who were callous and arrogant with no sense of responsibility and that their kind shouldn't go unpunished anymore. They started abusing us but no one tried to help the man who was still lying on the street, sound asleep, totally oblivious to the commotion he had caused.

One inquired 'Are you blind?'

The other said 'Must be. Because they have money.'

The third said 'Brahmins' and spat on the ground.

Still another hissed 'No Moustaches'

The fact that we could have been Brahmins (we were not) and were fair, had no moustaches but wore glasses and expensive clothes had fomented such a volcano of resentment that I (intellectual to the end), remember thinking at that moment how utterly kafkaesque all this was. In their inarticulate anger they had eloquently stated everything they held against our kind, the centuries of prejudice and repression and then the sudden half-baked empowerment called democracy which in actuality didn't mean a thing except for a blanket or two just before the elections.

No one had dared to lift their hands yet. It was still 1990 and Patna was predominantly upper class but in couple of years the equations would change. They were waiting for a sign. No one wanted to start it but would join in gleefully once it happened. I had almost gone into a deep shock. My hands were numb, the knees shaking badly, my heart in a cage of ice.

Anupam though still had his wits about him. He started abusing them back. At times like this retaliation is the only way out. Theatricality and melodrama, raised voices work but reasoning and logic never. Reasoning breeds counter bravado and makes even the weak feel strong.

Perhaps only a minute had passed, maybe less in which all this melodrama had been enacted and the man who was the sleeping partner to all this chaos suddenly with a groan woke up, startled to find so many people crowding over him gave a great howl of fright and in turn startled the mob. This was the opportunity that Anupam needed and he started the scooter, running it over the sprawled bicycle and couple of toes and we escaped. Some one yanked my hair from behind and in the bargain I lost couple of my precious locks. The hair still hasn't grown back in that part of my scalp as yet. The price some pay for wearing glasses and not wearing moustaches in Patna.

Like Osker, I wished I too had a drum to beat out my anguish. Maybe now after all these years I have finally got my drum.

Five minutes later standing outside my home, we were back to our old smart-ass selves. Both of us refused to acknowledge that we were horribly frightened. Till then we had lived a life of privilege and plenty and nothing there had prepared us for this. The cliche 'Was this the sign of things to come' echoed in both our minds and I remember scrutinizing the face of the labourer who came to work in our garden the next Sunday very hard but of course I couldn`t be sure. Earlier I had never noticed him. Now I did.

Anupam said 'Let's make a movie about this. A short movie. Half an hour, twenty minutes, you know something like *zero for conduct* or *An occurrence at owl creek.*'

'What shall we call it?' I asked him playing along. Those days we were always talking about making movies. We were a team. Like De Sica and Zavatini, Schrader and Scorsese, Sahir and Guru Dutt.

'How about "Patna Melodrama"?'

I thought it was corny and said so, then suggested an even more cornier one 'How about "A Scene from class struggle in Patna"?'

And Anupam's face broke into a dreamy smile 'Yes, yes, yes' and he cupped his hand around his right eye like a viewfinder and panned to my face lighting a cigarette and then panned left towards the empty street. A long shot. The deep silence, fine mist, a construction site, a group of labourers huddled around a fire, shivering. Cliches galore. The cloyingly sweet whiff of ganja in the air and then the music rolls out, building in tempo with the credits in Dolby sound. The light dims in the auditorium. The movie begins....

THE LEADER OF MEN

He was one of the replacement guards that came to work in our apartment building at the end of November. There are four guards in residence at all times. Two of them work in the daytime and the other two at night. They stay in poky little servant quarters near the parking lot and are not allowed to keep their families in there. Most of these security guards are lazy miserable fellows who are, it seems, just content to survive somehow. Most of them are illiterate and of the lower castes and amidst the gleaming chrome of the shining cars their poverty stands out in glaring contrast.

So I was taken by surprise when I first saw Roop Singh last December when I was back in Patna for the winter vacations. He wasn't at all like the other guards. He was around 5'10", well built, had a long sharp patrician nose and glorious light brown moustache that covered the upper lip and curled at the ends in a defiant flourish. He did credit to his name. His uniform was always ironed and creased and the shoes were gleaming black. He was so different from his defeated little brethren in mismatched uniforms and dusty brown keds that he was actually a revelation in the true sense of the word. He simply didn't fit in at all.

So, the first time I saw him he was at the reception counter in the lobby and was getting a dressing down from Mr. Kedia. Mr. Kedia lives right across our flat in F-9 and is in his late thirties. He has sundry business interests and is reputed to be fairly rich. He has the stupid arrogance that comes with it and he wears it on his face with the same sense of pride as the hideous chunky gold watch on his left wrist and the Motorola cell phone on his right hip. He is short and stocky and going bald. His face has started to bloat from excess of Stroh's beer. He is the kind of on the make, ready to take, upwardly mobile enterprising men, whom we see hovering around the periphery of our lives with alarming alacrity but then I guess it is a positive thing.

Kedia is the consummate consumer. A true child of his times. He has to buy things randomly to live, to survive, to find a purpose for his life. When he consumes he lives. Buying is his brand of nirvana. If a new car is not launched in the next six months he may simply fold up and die.

Back to the story now. There was Roop Singh standing

behind the counter and Kedia in front of him shouting and another man, who looked just like Kedia, gold watch and all, gesticulating frantically and shouting in the same breath. They were both very angry with Roop for some reason or the other. Normally I wouldn't have stopped because every few days or so Kedia shouts at one worker or the other. He is the president of the owner's association and he takes it very seriously. But it was Roop – his open confident face and erect bearing, an innate pride in himself, the sense of defiance and wounded honour in his eyes that made me pause and look over the scene in a new light. A totally astonishing thing happened then. Roop said to Kedia, 'But it is not my fault sir, I was just doing my duty,' in impeccable English, albeit with a little lilt of a rustic accent. Now this is wonderful I thought, I could suddenly sense drama in the lazy December air. Kedia is stupefied and he can't believe he has heard right and nor can his friend (for it has to be his friend). I can deduce it from the shock on their faces. The rights of snobbery have suddenly been reversed. I am sure Roop too can see it in their eyes. I am interested now but I realise how trivial the problem really is. Kedia is now all red in the face and bluster breaks out of it like hot air from a punctured balloon.

'You talk *English* to me! How dare you talk?'

'I just said that I was doing my duty, and I am not a rascal. I do understand English.' Roop said to Kedia in Hindi.

'I will kick you out.'

Roop kept quiet at this and contained in his anger but just barely.

I intervened around this time with a neutral 'What's the matter Mr. Kedia?'

He turned and looked at me. Normally he doesn't ever acknowledge my presence but that day I could see he was glad that I was there. He thought of me as an ally against the class enemy but soon I would prove to be the contrary.

'Ah Ritwik, good you are here,' he started to speak in English but I guess better sense prevailed and he switched over to Hindi, which was worse than his English but anyway 'My friend Mr. Sharma (here the man smiled and I smiled back), came to see me fifteen minutes back and this idiot of a guard wouldn't let him come up to my place.'

'I come here every week and this has never happened to me before. He wanted me to talk to Mr. Kedia over the intercom and when I refused he physically stopped me from going upstairs.'

I felt embarrassed in being involved with something as stupid as this but still I said ' He was only doing his duty and moreover he is new and doesn't know you.'

'He insulted my guest,' Kedia shouted but there wasn't much conviction in his voice anymore.

'These rules have been made by us Mr. Kedia, and Mr. Singh was only doing what he has been told to do and it is for your own safety.'

Sharma and Kedia glared at me and then Kedia said, 'Ritwik I am going to complain to your father. You don't even know how to talk to your elders.' I smiled at him and kept quite. He went away hurriedly into the elevator with his friend in tow. I took the stairs.

Later on I learnt from Munna, my servant, that his name was Roop and that he was a Rajput. Munna also told me that the other guards didn't like him much and thought him to be haughty and stuck up. He thought this was because Roop was of a ' forward' caste, all the others being ' backwards'. He generally kept to himself and after his duties were over read books in the guard room. All this seemed, to Munna, as subversive behaviour but even he grudgingly agreed that he was the best ever security guard that had worked at our building. He was smart, efficient and did his job quietly and competently and for this he got the princely sum of six hundred rupees a month and subsisted on boiled rice and potatoes like the other guards. All this for mere six hundred rupees a month, my shirts cost much more than that, it was ridiculous – the sum – but it was true.

Kedia did complain to my father but my father didn't say anything to me like I knew he wouldn't. But after that incident Kedia with his wounded pride came down hard on Roop Singh. He criticised Roop for everything and anything. He called him inefficient and insolent and once claimed that he had caught him sleeping at night while on guard duty. He was bent on getting him kicked out of the place but the other residents opposed the move and so Roop stayed.

Kedia just couldn't take the fact that a poor miserable little guard had answered back to him and that too in English. He was sure it was just to show him up in the front of his friend and worse, me. He was really sore about the 'English' part.

In his blind vanity he probably never even realised that he could have been wrong. He had always been rich and rich are always right; according to him there could be no two ways about it. Roop on his part didn't do anything that was counter reactionary except that he stopped saluting Kedia. Whenever someone else would be with Kedia, he would salute the other person but ignore Kedia, and this galled him no end.

It was during those days that that I came to know more about Roop from talking with him every evening for ten-fifteen minutes after I returned home. He felt obliged to me and later thanked me for my intervention that 'fateful' day. The other guards by that time had started to come around. Roop would read to them from the newspaper and tell them what was happening around the world; not that they were much interested. They had unofficially elected him to be their leader and I thought that it was fitting for he came from a race that were once leaders of men, warriors. His ancestors must have waged wars against the British and the Mughals and fought glorious battles amidst the golden sand dunes of Mewar. I think I am needlessly romanticising him, probably his ancestors were as poor as he was and were simple farmers toiling hard for their daily meal but who knows?

He was an educated person. He had studied till the intermediate from the College of Commerce, Patna, the very same college I had gone to albeit for a short time and much later than him. I didn't tell him that because I thought it might embarrass him. His father who was a farmer had died around that time and Roop had to leave his studies and look for a job. He went back to farming when he couldn't find any job that he liked. They didn't have much land and some of it had to be sold for his sister's wedding. He himself had married when he was just 15 and now had a wife and a son back home in the village. The income from the farm wasn't much so he left farming to his younger brother, who wasn't much interested in education anyway and started looking for a job again. Eventually he got a job as a teacher in a school near Bihta but after six months without pay and with no hope of the situation ever changing he left the job and came to Patna, drifting from job to job, sometimes working as a sales help in a grocery store, sometimes as a construction worker. Finally around four months back he had got the job with the security agency. He would tell me all these things without even an ounce of self pity yet I could feel the helplessness beneath his practised stoicism. He hadn't seen his family in six months and sometimes it made him deeply melancholic.

For a man of his background he was amazingly aware and

well read. He loved reading and often would talk to me about books that he had read and what he had felt about them. His perception was remarkably acute. I realised his was a sharper critical faculty than mine even though I am a student of literature. Perhaps because my experience of life has largely been vicarious while his I am sure has been more 'lived in' comprehensive one.

Though I am not as well read in Hindi literature as I want to be I have some books and these I lent to him. Among the books were a collection of Muktibodh's poems, the complete short stories of Renu and Dinkar's *Rashmi-Rathi*. He returned the Muktibodh back the very next day.

In the evenings when there would be no one in the lobby we would sit on the bench that was there and talk about the books and stories and life in general, little informal chitchat until I finished my cigarette and went back home upstairs.

Around that time he stopped saluting me and I was glad that he had stopped. Somehow it had always made me vaguely uneasy. After all we were not in the army.

He had one sweater that he would wear all the time. A bright maroon one that his wife had sent and he wore it with much pride over his grey uniform.

In the last week of December he sent a letter to my father asking for an advance of 100 rupees, which should be cut from his next month's salary because he suddenly had to send money home and now was in dire need of it in order to survive. He had written that he hadn't eaten anything for two days and now was having difficulty in doing his shift. It was a short, formal, very official letter.

Father had gone out so I went down with the money and gave it to him and also sent some food with Munna for him and the other guards.

When Kedia came to know he laughed at my naiveté and called Roop a lazy free loader. He thought aloud that probably Roop and other guards drank at night because he had heard noises sometimes and that is where all the money went. I kept quite.

Kedia is a devout man. He gives donations to temples, organises Jagrans regularly and himself performs Puja for an hour every morning but strangely enough has no faith in any other human being. Sometimes I wonder what kind of God he believes in. It must be the God of small things!

On 31st night a big bonfire and party was organised on the terrace of our apartment building. Since I am not a very social type I hadn't gone up to join the party but instead I watched Michelangelo Antonioni's wonderful *Blow-up* on cable T.V. My parents came home by 11 p.m., and much before the old year had rung out and the New Year rung in the party had died a cold lingering death. Many families had failed to turn up, and like it always happen at these things, more food than needed had been ordered and was now left untouched on the tables. Great heaps of Chicken and Meat and Biryani and Paneer and

Kofta curry, Gulab Jamun with no one to consume it all. The ladies came down by 11.30 and the remaining gentlemen drunks were in no position to stand let alone eat.

Anyway, one of the gentlemen drunks suddenly felt in his breast the milk of human kindness and said to Munna, who was there watching the antics and mixing the drinks and having a few pegs of his own, I am sure, 'Munna beta go downstairs and bring the guards up to eat, someone has to eat these damn things.'

So Munna went downstairs and the guards came up and all of them except Roop gorged on the food and went downstairs satisfied. Two of them had upset stomachs the next morning. As Roop picked up the plate and started to serve himself Kedia rolled over to him and said loudly, 'So Mr. Singh, I hope you are not hungry now. You probably haven't eaten such fabulous food ever in your life so eat carefully, don't overdo it.' And then he laughed and patted Roop on the back patronisingly. Roop felt as if someone had lit a long abandoned fuse inside his body and that it was snaking up slowly to his brain. He quietly put the plate down and walked away, aware of everybody's eyes boring into his back. The other guards chose to ignore Roop's reaction; they enjoyed themselves to the full.

What happened next can only be called unfortunate, maybe tragic but 'tragic' has a kind of grandeur attached to it, which doesn't necessarily include the minor characters of this world. Roop was on night duty, on the 31st of December. After the party had died down and people gone to sleep Roop sat in the lobby and brooded about what had happened. This is all reconstruction, all conjecture on my part, because the evidence is all physical and doesn't really say anything about his mind, except that he was perhaps hopelessly melancholic and full of hurt and pain. He probably thought about his family. About his no good brother, but a loyal one nevertheless, his beautiful wife who still looked young inspite of it all and his beloved land, his own little field of wasted dreams, on a part of which a bright red flag with a hammer and sickle had appeared suddenly one day and a small chunk of land was lost to him forever. As if by magic. He remembered he had cried that night holding his wife tightly and she too crying silently and their son sleeping serenely by their side. It was his son's beautiful calm face that made him go out in the morning and leave the village. It was his son's face again, that night, around four o'clock in the morning that finally upset the delicate balance of his mind. With his bare hands he ripped the lobby apart. With his fists he broke the glass revolving doors, the wooden bench where we sat and talked, the red plastic chairs and the intercom system. His hands were bleeding badly, the fingers broken at many places, and when Haripal, the other guard that night tried to stop him he punched him in the mouth. He was totally oblivious to pain, and only when Haripal came back with the other two guards and they all beat him up that he became quiet. But by that time the lobby was totally trashed. Haripal came to inform us and my father woke me up and we went downstairs. Some other residents followed in a little while. Roop was in the guardroom. They had tied him up with a rubber hose pipe. His face was swollen and his hands were badly smashed. The eyes were blank, expressionless, like the eyes of people we sometime see in B.B.C. documentaries in some remote corner of the world struck by natural disaster – an earthquake, a drought or a cyclone. I untied his hands and legs but he sat there on the floor motionless. Kedia didn't come down. Later I knew why he didn't. My father and few other residents took Roop to a nursing home nearby. He had multiple fractures on his hands .He probably would never work with his hands again. Damaged beyond repair. We have sued the security agency. Someone has to pay for the damages, I guess.

HARD BOILED

Outside the rain lashed down hard on the soft muddy street and inside the steamy sweaty room we lay silently on the mussed up bed breathing slowly but evenly. The windows are closed and the rain drops splash on the blue windowpane and blur the panorama. I light the first post-coital cigarette of the afternoon.

The smoke glides in and opens up like a fist in my lungs making me hollow from inside. She always cuddles up and curls unto me like a cat after we have made love – today she is distant yet. She is reluctant to forgive me for some unspecified crime but I do not want to go deep into it. I am already contrite.

I want her to curl up unto me and to enter me and be a part of my everything, fill up the hollowness, bone to bone, skin to skin, tissue to tissue, heart to heart, prick to pussy but a strange stubbornness gently binds me down. Today I want a time-out. I am not in a mood for the game. More and more nowadays, with alarming regularity I feel this way, like I am steeling myself from some dark adversity.

Why do I feel the need to protect myself against someone I love? But there you are, I do feel the need and so I don't inquire. I feign indifference. The raindrops look blue through the glass and their rhythmic tipptty-tapetty-tapettu-too add a strange stillness to our minds. I look at her.

She in turn is looking at her outstretched palms, perhaps trying to trace the fortunes of her future life through the criss crossing lines of her destiny. She doesn't believe in these things, I know. But it is different today. She is sad again. Infinitely sad and sadness does fuck up our mental equilibrium. I can feel it. It comes out of her body like mild effluvia mixed with fresh sweat. A salty blue perfume.

I notice she hasn't done her underarms for a long time now and the fuzz has turned ochre near the roots. Tiny beads of sweat cling to it like pearls on a string. It mildly arouses me.

After a while she turns her head .The eyes are awash with tears now.

She asks me slowly, her decibel level almost inaudible. I have to lip read. ' Do you really love me?' She asks and I turn my face away. She slides her head away from my outstretched arm.

Do I? Love her that is. Of course .Why the bloody theatrics? We are both so happy together, aren't we? But I keep silent. There is nothing to say really except to reiterate the obvious but suddenly I don't feel upto it. Any moment now I know the tears would start to roll down, a thin continous stream.

A sense of gloom has wafted over the whole place. A pure blue funk of ennui and despair. Her hands are folded over her breasts now, one knee curled up towards the turquoise wall. All taut smoothness and dull sheen.

She is beautiful. Of course I love her. But why is it today that we find simple speech so tortuous? Seemingly nothing has changed from yesterday or last week or even last year but something has, nevertheless.

Maybe she didn't have any orgasm; today she didn't even pretend to fake it. I always get cruel when I am angry and I am cruel to people I love but then that is no consolation, not to me and certainly not to her. Her mouth, lips and tongue get very soft when she nears her climax but today it had retained its secular warmth throughout.

'You never seem to feel anything deeply. Nothing is important to you. Everything is a big joke. Our whole life, the future, a home, a real home, is a joke to you. You feel nothing.' She tries hard not to sound angry and defeated. The nipples stiffen from the strain, the tears flow out.

It is not true but what can I say? I feel miserable but I also feel an intense desire to laugh out this pain into oblivion. Wipe the slate clean. But if I do that, I know she will take it as yet another example of my flippant attitude towards everything sacred in general.

I don't blame her. Anyone would feel the same. She stares at the wall.

Her back is towards me. I try to draw her unto me. Fold her into my arms, smoothen her sweat clotted hair. It makes her break out into a fresh batch of tears – the strongest hydraulic force in the world.

She feels totally alone. Abandoned. She is terrified. I can sense it because I myself have felt it many times. On some dark days, at one time or the other, we all feel abandoned, forsaken, like orphans. Then loneliness looms large like a giant octopus, its tentacles reaching every corner of our meagre world. Tears are good at times like this. At least it gives one something to do. It keeps you occupied.

'Why do you say that? Have I ever let you down? Am I not there for you always?' I ask her half knowing the answer, sure of my stance. I know I am not in the wrong.

'You are always so distant. Closed up like a shell. What are you afraid of?'

'Nothing.' I say and I am right.

'Let's face it you are indifferent to everything except sex. There is not much difference between you and a quadruped. You never tell me about anything and I discuss everything with you, every single fucking thing but you ....' And here she makes a vague fluttering motion with her hands. Her hands are beautiful, slender long fingers which are soft yet surprisingly strong. Writerly hands but she doesn't write, except for memos. She weaves patterns of intricate beauty while she talks .It was one of those numerous things that drew me to her in the old days. I guess it is her turn to be cruel now.

'I tell you everything that you need to know'

'Need to know (here she shouts), what does this suppose to mean? I want to know everything. Don't you know everything about me?'

'Yes I do'. I tell her softly but do I?

'Then why not me? Why do you keep your thoughts so secret? Why is everything so covert? An espionage, a subterfuge, a secret venture up a dark alley?'

I smile now. It is the least I can do. It is so strange how sometimes everything pure and bright can transform itself into the raw and the rotten in such a short while.

I playfully run my hand up her naked leg and she jerks it away with a look of sheer disgust. Now I am really really angry. This is taking it a bit too far We all have our bouts of intense melancholia but that doesn't mean ... no sex!

'You have five minutes to dress up and leave,' I hiss at her, secure in the knowledge that she will dissolve into a quivering column of tears and bury her head into my hairy chest. And everything would be fine. All said and done, I don't have a heart of stone. I too am a sensitive man.

I wash the dishes after dinner. Sometimes.

Then a strange thing happens or maybe it is my imagination. She looks at me and the colour of her eyes change and in them flash across something that I have only seen once before in my life. I remember I was thirteen and I had just beaten the neighbour's cat so hard that it lay on the ground motionless. Its breathing was irregular or totally absent. I don't recall, but I was fascinated and felt proud and excited. I remember I almost had a hard-on. Out of sheer excitement I knelt beside the cat and poked her with a stick. She was dying. And then her eyes jerked open and she snarled and hissed and leapt at me. Like traffic lights the colour of her eyes changed to red from green and in them flashed across something that I would see once more, in the luminous eyes of my intended, years later. Just now.

She swings her legs slowly and pulls up her panties, picks up the bra slung from the chair like a slingshot, puts on her blouse, drapes the sari, puts on her pearls and slips on her ring, elegant and cool as ever. Within five minutes too. The stipulated time. She opens the door and on her way out closes it softly. Without a backward glance. She doesn't even slam the fucking door.

For a long time I lie there, naked and feeling increasingly stupid. Tossing restlessly, totally numb till I feel a sharp tearing pain in my backside. I turn over and feel my bum. There is something embedded in the fleshy part of the right cheek.

There is blood on the sheet. A jagged splinter of her shattered Shankha. There are pieces of ivory strewn all over the bed. Fuck. The sight of blood nauseates me. I faint.

WILL YOU BE MY VALENTINE?

Some one was calling out her name softly and incessantly from between the hollows of a beautiful ruined tomb and tugging at her blanket but it felt like it was happening to someone else in some distant dream, twice removed from her and reality. She burrowed deep inside the thick blanket and slept on contentedly but after a while she felt the blanket being snatched from her and reluctantly she opened her eyes, she felt cold and she curled up her bare legs and tried to focus her eyes to the shape looming above her.

'Wake up angel, wake up, wake up. I have been trying to wake you for the past ten minutes, Don't you want to wake up early today, today! today! today! today!' It was her roommate Ritu, Anjali could make out after a few seconds of repeated blinking-unblinking and adjusting to the dim darkness.

She was still feeing very sleepy and now very bugged.

'Why? What is so important about today? Go back to sleep' she squinted at her watch. 'It is only eight o'clock and really what is so important about today. It is here this time of the week every year, with monotonous regularity,' Anjali said quietly and pulled up the blanket again. Ritu sat down beside her on the bed and started doing her nails. She had already taken her bath and her long hair was all wet and shampooed and hung down to her waist in shiny thick waves.

'It is Valentine's day today, if you remember angel.' Everyone in the hostel called Anjali angel because she was very tiny and delicate and also because 'angel' kind of went with Anjali who was always very nice and sweet to everybody.

At first she used to feel very uncomfortable when someone called her that because she explained to everybody, 'it makes me feel like a symbol of some kind or the other,' but it persisted and the name stuck on and now she didn't mind it really, it was such better than being called 'tinytoes,' or 'Babyfinger' or worse still 'Babydoll'!

'Right, Valentine's day', lover's day, oh yes how can I forget? Have I not been waiting all these months for today? For just this one glimpse of 'today'? Of course I have been oh yes, but still it is too early for me'.

'All right but I just thought I should wake you up, you don't want to be late for Ritwik, do you?'

'No I won't be late I told him I would be there by eleven,

I won't be late.'

'He has sent such beautiful cards to you, really lovely ones, Ritwik is a real romantic guy. A bonafide knight in shining armour,' Ritu winked at her and Anjali couldn't help smiling, Ritu was wearing her new lace underpants and she caught her looking at her and she wiggled her bottom at Anjali and winked again, and they both laughed.

'He is a real 'cool dude' Ritwik is.' Anjali said softly and slowly she got up from the bed and the floor felt cold and slippery to her feet and she walked on her toes to where she had thrown her slippers and slipped her feet into warm fur.

Ritu had changed into a soft red and white sari, the blouse was a bit loose and her arms looked thinner, Anjali went and assisted her in tightening up the blouse with a safety pin and straightened the fall of her sari and looked at her critically and lit a cigarette.

'No, no, don't wear that' bindi, that is too small, wear the big one and don't tie up your hair, yes the big one. It kind of looks more chic and bindaas,' She said to Ritu and dropped the ash on the floor.

'Nice?' Ritu asked her not really sure of the way she looked.

'You look beautiful.'

'Really?' she was smiling now and looked radiant and it made her look prettier than she was.

'Really' Anjali passed the cigarette to her.

'Ravi says that girls look better in saris, they look more "womanly," more grown up and mysterious.'

It is always 'Ravi says this, Ravi says that' thought Anjali to herself, a bit amused.

'You look womanly enough, don't worry,' Anjali said after a while.

'What will you wear? And for god sake don't wear that grungy pair of jeans, you look like a little kid in those, wear something traditional.' Ritu said seriously to her and exhaled a lungful of blue gray smoke and passed the cigarette back to Anjali.

'I have no problem in looking like a kid. I am a kid, remember? I have hardly grown up, I have always been a kid, right since childhood. And I love that pair of jeans.'

'Not today, wear something nice, Ritwik will love it, okay, angel, okay?'

'All right, I will wear that cream salvarsuit of mine.'

'Yes, do that. I must hurry, I have to get to Vasant Kunj, he is staying with his mausi and from there we will drive out.' Ritu said a bit breathlessly and looked for the last time at the mirror and straightened her sari for the umpteenth time, she wasn't much comfortable with saries yet.

'Say hi to Ravi for me and have fun. See you at 7.30.' Anjali said to Ritu who was at the door now.

'You too and listen, say hi to Ritwik and give a big kiss to him from me bye.' Ritu said breathlessly and she was gone.

Anjali crushed the cigarette on the floor and then she picked up the butt and put it carefully in an envelope filled chock full with other butts and put it behind her books, away from view.

Suddenly she felt very forlorn and for a few seconds passed into a pure blue funk of melancholia but then she caught sight of her image locked in the mirror and she couldn't help smiling. She looked so sad and blue that it was hilarious, sadness didn't go with her face. She was still smiling when she went inside the bathroom to wash.

She was in her second year studying literature and she was happy doing that. She liked literature, liked the eternal magic of stories and had always wanted to study it and she was good at it too but when she had first come to Delhi from Patna and stayed in the hostel, it was the first time she had stayed away from home and with so many girls and she had felt out of place with their sophistication and cool. She wasn't cool she knew that, she was just pretty and intelligent and all the other girls to her looked more beautiful, more intelligent, more aware and chic than her. She felt she couldn't compete with them, ever.

All those cool girls had boyfriends and those boys would come and visit the girls in the evening outside the hostel and she would look at them and wonder how do these girls meet these boys. Some of the boys looked really cute to her. She went to many college festivals, to seminars, to plays, where her new more experienced friends had hinted she could meet boys but nothing like that happened and so after a while she was reconciled to the philosophy 'there must be some magic, some mystery in it that is totally beyond my range.' She was content with the explanation but then one fine day after the last summer vacation Ritu, who was her best friend, a year senior to her and her roommate cum soulmate came and let it drop as unobtrusively as a fox in a chicken coop that she was wildly in love. Ritu had fallen in love with a guy called Ravi back in her hometown during the vacation, he was studying at I.I.T. Kanpur and showed a snap of the boy to Anjali. He was good looking, very handsome in fact, Anjali had to admit that.

Ritu who had always bitched about those girls who had boyfriends and had a kind of condescending attitude towards them, had herself gone ahead and fallen in love. Anjali had a curious sense of dismay over this and then she had felt guilty about it.

Ritu would read aloud all her love letters to Anjali when they would arrive and moon over Ravi's snap at night. She kept it underneath her pillow. Ritu would in her cupid induced stupor tell her 'You should fall in love, too angel, you don't know what you are missing'. Life got unbearable for Anjali but she smiled on, like always.

So when she went home in the autumn break, there in the sanctuary of her room, she created 'Ritwik'. She had always liked the magic of stories. She worked hard on Ritwik. She made notes on him and carved him out solid and real from the limpid block of her fertile imagination.

1. Ritwik should study at J.N.U. and should be 2-3 Years older than her.
2. He is a close friend of her cousin's.
3. She met him at her cousin's place during the vacation and it was kind of love at first sight for them.

Ritu would like that, she liked 'love at first sights'. These were the main points and she added little bits of detail to go with it. She selected a snapshot of the cousin standing underneath a tree with some of his friends laughing and saying something and there was a guy sitting indolently on a mobike, looking away from the camera. He had a remote quality and it struck the right note to Anjali. She picked him up to be her Ritwik. When she asked her cousin what his name was, he wasn't sure because that guy wasn't such a good friend of his. So Anjali called him 'Ritwik' because it kind of went with the image she had of him and also most importantly she had no idea what Ritwik really meant. It was okay, it wasn't a great characterization but it would do.

So when she came back from her vacations, she acted a bit mysterious for a few days and when Ritu and her other friends were sufficiently riled, she coyly confided to them that she was in love with a J.N.U. intellectual named Ritwik and showed them the snapshot. In a few days the news spread like wildfire in the hostel and the girls smiled at her and gave her meaningful looks. She liked that. Like all artists she loved applause. Everything was fine now and even Ritu didn't moon that much anymore. Once in a while she disappeared for a day and spend it watching movies at Priya and be back by 7.30 and announce in a cool manner that she had lots and lots and lots of fun with Ritwik.

She looked at her watch, it was 9.30 now. Time to move on, she said to herself. She pulled on her 'grungy' pair of jeans and a black turtle neck sweater, combed back her short hair and put on her glasses and she went out.

The college wore a festive look, most of the girls were decked up and had bunches of roses in their hands and their faces were shining with excitement. The whole university was alive to the beat of lovers hearts. Hunks with slicked back hair and sunglasses moved around in shiny cars in a desperate manner and girls were bunched in groups outside the colleges, cool and waiting to be plucked. It was a festival on par with any of the real festivals, perhaps now more important than them. Anjali felt nauseous with all the gaiety flying around unchaperoned mixed with exhaust fumes. She caught the bus for Priya. One really good thing she felt had come out of this charade, she had become a serious movie buff. She always found silver linings where there was none.

She reached Priya round 11.15 and she got the ticket for the afternoon show. They were still showing *Alladin*, she had already seen it thrice. The crowd of happy people was there too and she realised it wasn't such a great idea to visit Priya on Valentine's day. Some of the girls from the hostel could be there or worse still Ritu and Ravi could drop in, after all Ravi was visiting for a few days and would surely like to see *Alladin* and on what better day to watch it than on Valentine's day, right?

She was one of the first to get inside the hall and settled comfortably in the back and the movie started. She liked Alladin, he was very handsome and had beautiful dark eyes and she would have loved to be his princess. At the interval when the lights came on she got the shock of her life. Ritu and Ravi were sitting just three rows in front of her. There was a big group of kids with them. Probably friends of Ravi thought Anjali and crouched low in her seat and heaved a big sigh of relief when the lights were turned off again but she couldn't enjoy the movie any longer. The pizza she had eaten before the show sat in the middle of her belly like a big sticky mass of lump.

Just five minutes before the ending the group got up, three girls and two boys and Ravi, only it wasn't Ravi as Anjali could make out in the flickering light. It wasn't Ravi at all. The group went out and Ritu was still sitting there, her eyes glued to the screen.

That guy wasn't Ravi, from a distance in her excitement he had seemed – now everything become clear to her.

When the movie ended and the crowd moved out, Ritu

was in the front, walking a little awkwardly in her beautiful red-white sari, getting curious stares from the cool kids. She looked so beautiful and alone that it broke Anjali's heart. Some of the magic died for her them.

At night after dinner, Ritu came into the room. She looked serene, calm and satisfied. Anjali didn't look at her. She was staring at the ceiling.

'Why didn't you come to the mess for dinner?'

She asked Anjali in an off hand manner.

'Just didn't feel like eating'.

'Ravi and I had such a great time today. he was really romantic and beautiful today. we went to Surajkund.' She said to Anjali softly while brushing her hair and Anjali suddenly realised that Ritu wasn't putting up an act. She wasn't lying in her heart.

'Even we went to Surajkund.'

Ritu's eyes flickered once and she turned and looked at Anjali and smiled.

'Really? it is such a pity we missed each other, it is always so crowded. We could have had such a great time together me and Ravi, you and Ritwik.'

'Yes,' Anjali whispered.

'Aren't we lucky we have someone we can hold on too, some one who loves us as much as we love them,' Ritu said softly and smiled beautifully.

'Yes,' Anjali accepted and lit a cigarette.

THE LONELINESS OF THE SHORT STORY WRITER

I have measured out my life in large patiala pegs, and frankly my love it sucks. I sit here day after day with a pen in my hand, a blank virginal pages staring right into my eyes unable to come alive and I think it has all come to a waste. The slide from the land of gup to the land of chup has been swift and definitive. There are no stories anymore to tell. I despair – but a tiny voice at the back of my mind pipes up now and then with a 'it's not true, not true at all'. There always will be stories as a long as there is life but somehow it all comes out as stillborn. Dead on arrival. The last story I did was couple of months back when we were together. When I would just pick up a pen and point it to the page and a world all tangible and new would appear and we could escape into it and be safe from the encroaching reality. My love, come back to me. I know I have sinned. I am consumed with remorse. Be an angel and grant me absolution.

Each dawn I awake, and for half an hour I lie back on the bed, eyes open, staring at the ceiling fan unable to get up – no drowsiness or anything but just the complete lack of will to get up and face what I dread to face. I do the mandatory fifty pushups and crawl to the table. It is piled up with books, many I haven't touched in weeks, maybe months. Large tomes of wisdom no doubt but even these do not alleviate the utter sense of desolation that I feel. I sit in my chair, pick up the pen that you had given me, a silver mont blanc long back I remember it like it was yesterday, right here in my little barsati with the dark green walls. You remember that don't you? It's the same pen with which I write today this lament to my soul. The notepads are there, expensive and blank, the finest money can buy, at the corner squats the old Remington.

Above the table on the wall hangs a lithograph of a man who was once to me the embodiment of all that I wanted to be, in his eyes freedom and rebellion blaze like slow fire, the face undeniably angelic with the prettiest lips on any man that I have seen. Prettier than Presely, a tougher Montgomery Clift with the same brooding sadness; and what glorious talent while it lasted. It is old Jack Kerouac who looks to me from the wall everyday but St. Jack, kind Jack, free Jack, has no accusation in his eyes Jack. Hey Jack, thou prince of the beat and the beat-up, thou saint of love and loneliness, help thine acolyte mired in misery, wallowing in wine, soaked up with self pity, miserably maudlin to boot. Just show me the open road mate and I will go. The backpack is ready. It is also empty. But he with his beatific smile can't help me anymore, he has been dead for 30 years now, a drink sodden death straining at the toilet seat ... no sorry I apologise that was Elvis. I am getting my stories confused. Jack died watching the tube, washed up and dead for years when he died. You frighten me Jack but still I love you Jack. I wanted his freedom, his words, his mind, hell I wanted to be a rebel too. I longed to be alienated too. He was poor and I was rich, he hated his father and I loved mine, he had a chip on his shoulder and I wanted one too. Till one day as the mist cleared I met you and wanted to conform to everything that you projected. You brought out the bohemian beneath the bourgeois, the snake beneath the skin, the artist behind the thick-lensed dullness in me. Jack with the pack on his back, a smile on his lips and a backward glance and a wink that said 'You are in good hands brother, just hold tight,' went up the lonely road; pather panchali playing upon his tongue unforked. I didn't complain, I had you and I could write.

It was heaven. All those years I would always think of writing about you. Construct a veritable home movie of a story about you but never could because for one I had other things to write about. You opened the floodgates of my mind and stories, poems, haikus came rushing out like vomit and there were only so many I could mop up; many spilled about everywhere in alcohol and friends and foolishness but I couldn't care less about it then. I was sure there would be more to follow. You were too real to write about. I couldn't ever distance myself from you. You were on my back like wings and in my side like eve in adam's rib. There was no getting away from you. You were the one thing that I kept just for myself. I couldn't have shared you with the world but I should have. I know that now. I should have bound you in words never to let you depart. I should have paid attention to Donne. I should have listened to him and you could still be here beside me watching the bloody sunne rise and go down again in the evening, drinking beer, comparing Larkin's 'Aubade' to Empson's. But I can start now and retrieve lost ground. I could write about the time when I first met you. Remember the fair? The stupid fair? The eternal fair? The book fair. Do you remember the two adolescents young with lust who barely could keep their hands off each other and wished to melt away together far away from the madding crowd – and they did. You remember that, don't you? I should have written about that. About your hair auburn and straight, uncombed and loose, symbol of disorder, 'chaos' my literary friends perhaps would call, and which I would shampoo and comb back from your high forehead but never braid. Even when you would come with your hair tightly bound in a bun I would close the door and take out the pins. Or your toe ring shining with silver sweat or the toe itself. The small left one. If not a short story perhaps a haiku,

Your bloody toe
in my mouth
taste of salt and sour metal.

See now I do it and it comes out all wrong. Remember the time I came pissed drunk to the hostel. I had published my first story and was delirious with joy, we had just met the other week and here I was on my knees and laughing and crying, all at the same time, and your friends were horrified but you had laughed when any other girl would have died of social apoplexy. Later on that night in the hostel, your roommate envious and scandalized, asked you 'So he writes. That's all very well but what does he plan to do exactly or is he as vella as you are?' and you replied, 'Well you saw didn't you?' and laughed some more.

Rifat, come back I still love you. Do you still keep the copy of my story on your desk, like you did when we were together or have flushed it down the toilet with the photograph and other memories?

I should have written about that, about finding in that laughter an affirmation of our oneness. We understood each other totally. We communicated silently, our fingers intertwined bashfully and to say nothing of our souls, walking together in the November chill, coffee in styrofoam cups from the hostel, the moon dirty and weary coming out at 5 'o' clock in the evening behind us. Your friends suspicious and protective and mine frankly bewildered – but we didn't care, did we? We talked about Art and commitment and all that jazz but more often than not we talked just about literature: Agyeya and Muktibodh, Barthelme and Carver, Rushdie and Marquez. We spent endless evenings discussing magic realism, dirty realism, neo-realism, oblivious to the world. Sometimes comparing the Hughes' crow to Laxman's series on crows and sometimes the dichotomy in Garfield's sloth to Macavity's feline stealth. One of those early courtship days I brought you a copy of *Gone with the Wind* because you mentioned that all your friends had read it upteen number of times and you wanted to see what the fuss was all about; but you could never finish it though you kept trying intermittently over the years. I never realized how much you hated the book until the 'incident' couple of months back.

You would always wear that frayed black jeans of yours, one that I totally detested and gray college sweat shirt with the hood pulled over your head and which made you look mysterious like Orco. It would be very hard to kiss you – I had to pull the hood down every time. Did you use your hood as a ghunghat silly girl? Come 7 'o' clock and you would say goodbye and I would protest 'we have half an hour more at least' and you would always say 'But I have a tutorial tomorrow'.

Or of the time we both met Arundhati Roy at the Delhi School of Economics cafeteria when she had come to lecture on *Bandit Queen* and how it was such an exploitative movie. She wasn't the goddess of all things then but just as lovely as ever and how I had made a fool of myself by disagreeing with her, making her angry in return, and I had not even seen the movie then, well nobody had. It hadn't been released yet but in retrospect I was right. You laughed all the way back to the hostel but you see I had to impress her. She was so lovely … though I agree she didn't take it kindly.

Once you won five hundred bucks in a poetry contest and we went to see *Death and the Maiden* with Bhaskar Ghosh in it. We bought the most expensive tickets available and later on had dinner in a Mexican restaurant and didn't have any money left for the auto fare. It was 10 o'clock in the night and we caught the 901 for the university. I had a fight with a couple of inebriated louts when they tried to act fresh with you.

The prudent thing to do would have been to get down and catch another bus but something made me fight. I wasn't scared then but I was, afterwards. When at home that night you said to me ' I was so scared man' and buried your face in my chest, I burst out crying myself. I was embarrassed afterwards and said to you 'I am just not the Macho type' and you said 'I would hate you if you were'. The next morning we had a good laugh over it with our morning chai and then you left because you had a tutorial.

We could laugh at anything then, love, happiness, sadness, humbug. We used laughter like a machete to level anything and everything. You had the bright idea to write a short story about it in collaboration with me, and as we spun it yard for yard it became in a short while a fit treatment for a movie by

Mrinal Sen on a bad wicket. Remember *Calcutta 71*?

My eyes lost focus for days after watching that.

It is good that I didn't write anything about it seriously because it never would have come out the way it happened. It would never have been a story but at best only an anecdote like it is now.

Once after reading *Ulysses* in two days flat I went blind one morning and panicked and also had high temperature and my only thought was to have you by my side and my old landlady, that sweet old lady, called you and you came running though you had a tutorial that day. You cooked for me, looked after me, took me to the doctor, brought the medicines and generally with cool efficiency took over and made me as good as new in only a couple of days time. Can I put that in a story and still tell you how blessed, how loved I felt? It is good I never wrote about that because, perhaps, then I would have destroyed it but I remember everything. Since you have gone I have suddenly got the curse of total recall.

One time we went to the Alliance Francaise to see Truffaut's *Jules et Jim* and but of course we didn't have the passes but we knew would get in and we did. We begged, we cajoled, we pleaded and flashed our college identity cards, did our 'sir we one students act' and and got in at last but since the chairs were all taken, we sat on the steps. Rich matrons in pearls cast us curious stares but we didn't mind. Later on I made you jealous by going on and on about how fascinating Jeanne

Moreau really was and I only stopped when you cried.

I never thought I would miss you so. The only comfort these days are those memories. They are with me everywhere, when I go to the library in the morning, when I am working on the stupid dissertation, at the dhaba nearby where I have my lunch everyday, and back home in my room from where it seems you have never left. At the corner of my table, beside the typwriter, the manuscript of your book of poems is kept. How well you write, I get jealous sometimes. Your poems are a great comfort, they speak to me in your voice and remind me of your wit and charm and dear comrade the last seminar we attended together. It was spring and Al Macguffin was giving a lecture at St. Stephens on 'post modernism', and as he came to speak the mike was perhaps a bit faulty and Macguffin as the klutz incarnate tried to position it right and in the process demolished it totally. A new one had to be brought and horror of horrors in that August snooty gathering your high pitched laughter proletarian suddenly rang out. I couldn't control the giggles myself. We were both thrown out. Later on you said, solemnly, as we sat in the coffee house that it was the single most defining act of 'deconstruction' that you had ever seen. I wished at that moment if only I had thought of it first but as usual you beat me to the gun. We had the big fight couple of days after that.

The only time my memory fails is when I think about that fateful day, about that stupid fight we had and everything comes through a wall of perforated mist; words, phrases and some actions are missing at times and my memory unspools through many jumpcuts. All I remember is that I played Othelo to your Desdemona with my mind at its scene stealing best as Iago. All I know is that I am sorry. I was a fool to suspect you of infidelity but you did praise Ritwik's story much more than mine at the café and he kept giving you those adoring looks of his while I burned up inside. His stories are better I agree now but I was consumed by envy then – and you shouldn't have shouted and thrown *Gone with the Wind* at me, smashed my glasses and I shouldn't have punched you and split open your lips and then for an encore given you a black eye, to say nothing of your hair a tuft of which somehow came into my hands in the end. I sincerely hope it hasn't made you bald in the back.

My fingers have atrophied since then, withered and scaly white like Chanticleer claws, though I can still hold a pen and write, like I do now, but the blood has dried up and believe me, even then as I hit you, I had realized that perhaps this time I had gone too far. But I didn't hit you out of spite or anger or to teach you a lesson but only out of artistic curiosity. Now I believe at the back of my mind the burning question was whether I could ever hit you or not? And how would it feel to hit? And to watch your face and gauge your emotions after the act closely so I could write about it later on. It was just an experiment darling. My anger had died out the moment before I had hit you. Just an experiment for my art, you see, I had never hit a woman before. I really never thought you would take it so badly and disappear totally from my life. I realize the enormity of my act and am now penitant. I am down on my knees and *begging baby please,* but I didn't do it for pleasure. I did for art and as an artist you too can understand the importance of investigation and experiment in the art of Method writing. Perhaps by now you too have written a long poem about it. You are my Beatrice, my Banalata Sen, my Layla. You are my own little private goddess of all things. Come back little Mira, come back to daddy, come back back back or let me do my Jimmy Dean in all my petulant surly mouth sorrow, 'YOU ARE TEARING ME APART, YOU ARE TEARING ME APART! That was always good for a laugh wasn't it darling? Back in the good old days but now it has become excruciatingly real and cuts right to the bone …

24

I am 24 years old today. A beautiful, wild, cheerful 24. The breasts are still firm. Upturned and perky. The tummy tucked and poster smooth. Hips delicate, made of glass. I am proud of my body. It is all class. The legs long, supple and strong. The heart a tired leonine. Tired? Why? Ritwik. That is why. I wish he would do something soon.

Anything. Earn some money. Settle down. So I can marry the slippery little bugger finally. For a certified intellectual he is incredibly stupid. No sense of reality at all. I want to mate now. The time is ripe.

Moreover I am bored. It would be a change, don't you think? There would be responsibilities no doubt but I am old enough, am I not? I can take care of anything. I have got a couple of baby cactuses on my desk and they haven't died in weeks. Also a nine months old dachshund, who is living yet.

It is early morning. Still dark with a hint of rain. Here in paradise.

Just kidding, of course, but on some days it really is like paradise. On those days we all love each other very much. Mama, Papa, Adolf and Mira. On other days it is like any other normal home. Then it is not fun at all. But then nobody ever said that parents were supposed to be 'fun' and families 'cool', did they? They are asleep. My parents. I have one clear hour of uninterrupted privacy yet. Before they awake.

I won't work on my dissertation today but in the afternoon go to the library and treat Ritwik to some magical omelettes and cold coffee at kaake da dhaba. I wish I could treat him to a nice juicy double pizza with sausage topping. Well, that would have to wait for now. The one good thing about Ritwik is that he eats anything. He is omnivorous. He consumes everything. Never complains. Just like Adolf. My sweet little portable liver breath sprayer. The only difference is that Ritwik smells better. Tastes good too. Well if he wants anything juicier than an omelette he can always suck on my tits later on behind the reference section. He tastes of jaggery. Ritwik does. Of jaggery with a twist of lime.

Before I knew Ritwik I thought the human body only smelt of abstract things at different times of day. Of security and concern like my father's hands in the evening when he would come home from work tired and soft, of loneliness in my arm-pit hair after another unending college 'social', of despair and fear on my mother's lips when on some empty sunfilled winter afternoon she would kiss my forehead and cry.

My parents don't like Ritwik much. I don't blame them. He is a bit of an oddity really. An acquired taste. But I love him don't I? That should be enough for them. That is if they really are my parents and haven't adopted me from the nearest orphanage. I don't look anything like my parents so you never know. That is one of my ever-recurring nightmares, really. On the other hand I think it is simply an overdose from the golden era of Hindi movies on the late night channel. The 70s. I have such a nostalgic thing for the 1970s. Perhaps it is because I was born then.

Love those printed polyester shirts, bell-bottoms and dog collars. Long hair, sideburns, and handlebar moustaches. Zeenie baby on a slow burn doing 'dum maro dum', kumbh ka melas, Manmohan Desai, and lost and found themes. Ah the 70s! It was the time when even God wanted to look like Amitabh Bachchan and often did. At least to me. Now not even Amitabh looks like Amitabh anymore. Talk about losing face. Literally.

'Mira, he doesn't have much of a future'. My mother told me once and I didn't talk to her for couple of days. She got the message. Loud and clear. Mama dear sweet Mama you don't leave anyone for something as slight as not having 'much of a future', for being of a different caste or community or religion, for being poor. It is almost like killing an infant in Rajasthan for turning out to be a girl.

It is deliberate cruelty. And like Blanche I won't ever be condemned for that. Perhaps his parents think about me in the same way. A klutzy anorexic girl full of intellectual pretensions come to whisk away their gorgeous tub of Dalda of a son. PARENTS! They are mostly right, of course. Because of hindsight. Because they too did some wrong in their youth. They call it experience. In youth the right to wrong is a fundamental right. I do not want to be devoid of my share. Perhaps in time Ritwik would turn out to be my tragic flaw. My 'hamartia'. Tell you what? I will take my chance for now.

The birds sing the aubade outside on the window sill. The house is stirring. I hear my father piss in the toilet bowl. He will come and wish me afterwards. Sweet sweet daddy. Mother is making coffee. Ah, the lazy bleary-eyed smell of strong espresso in the morning. And none makes it better than my mother. She mouths a silent 'Happy Birthday Darling' and blows me a kiss. Mira blows it back. I will do my yoga now and sing the body geometric. Must keep it supple and smooth for Ritwik. From the corner Adolf lets out a delicate fart and then ashamed pretends to be asleep. Just like Ritwik.

THE WRITER'S WIFE

Monday came at last, and with it, the letter. Finally. The verdict was out since last week. But Mira had somehow restrained herself from calling up the Magazine. She wanted the letter. In writing. Whether she won or lost. The short-story competition, that is. For posterity, it could become an important document. Like the Birth-Certificate. The School leaving certificate. The Death-Certificate. It would change the course of her life, so she wanted it in writing. She had plotted it that way. If she won she would leave Ritwik. Her husband. If she lost, well she would simply wait till the next contest. In the past one year she had already lost three. She closed the letter box. Let the letter lie there like a rattler. She would wait. Yet.

She was the writer's wife. That is her husband was a 'writer' or rather thought that he was a writer. He was actually just a middlingly successful book reviewer and society columnist who once in a while still wrote the occasional unpublished poem. For the last seven years he had been Casaubon-like working on the great Indian postmodern neo-magic realistic novel tentatively titled 'Magnum Opus' The old broken down refrigerator was already filled to bursting point with shrink packed yellow manuscript pages. He had started the novel on their honeymoon. In fact the first line had been written on Mira. Literally on her. From her belly button to her breasts. *It was a dark and stormy night.* Ritwik the writer. The boy whom all her friends had found darkly glamourous. In the final year of college. She wondered now if it had been a conspiracy all along. On her friends part. Her friends found him to be good looking, so Mira too decided that he was handsome. Her roommate found him interesting so Mira too started taking an interest in him. Then her best friend fell in love with him and Mira had no choice but to claim Ritwik for her own.

To be fair to Ritwik, he actually did have a modicum of subversive charm those days. He was different. When all the other boys were preparing for a M.B.A., he wrote poetry. On her. She should have known then. By the end of the first year he had published his first long short-story in a noted 'Little' magazine. He graduated, had a job with a newspaper and published his first very slim anthology of poems. They got married. He started work on the *Novel.* Things started getting fucked up after that. The short-stories stopped getting published. The poems limped back home rejected. The 'Little' magazines, the 'Slicks' all turned their backs on the golden boy.

Love went out quickly and cleanly from their marriage after that. It wasn't as if he was constantly abusive. He only hit her about once a week. After a while it just became hard for Mira to take on all those rejected stories and poems. She felt all those millions of words floating around her, slowly sucking out happiness right from her life. He wasn't even good looking anymore. She never forgave him that. That he was untalented she could somehow rationalize but the fact he let himself get fat, lose all his hair and with it in retrospect his erection galled her no end.

He would get drunk every second day and would chastise the literary world for the injustice of it all and cast aspersions on the critical acumen of all the editors in the trade. After the sixth peg he would start on the novelists 'Ah Rushdie, now there's a bugger with no ....' and Mira would clamp her hands over her ears. Ritwik would hit her then. A back hand cross-court. But the worst was that then he would cry the whole night and not let her sleep. Like most literary minded married women all over the world, Mira too couldn't fathom how the golden boy straight out of F. Scott Fitzgerald, that she had gone to bed with, somehow turned into a Stanley Kowalski in the morning. Worse, he didn't even look anywhere like Brando.

She decided to leave him finally. But she wouldn't go gently. She would wound him first. She would be successful where he failed. She started writing and found to her surprise that it came naturally to her. Mira started sending contributions to short-story contests, and when the letters would come she would leave them unopened in the letter box. She would watch from behind the curtain as Ritwik opened the letter and read. The reaction on his face would decide his fate. For the last three times continuing it had been uncontrollable mirth which had carried on through the night. Intermittently.

Come 4' o'clock and the doorbell rang. Ritwik scuttled in. 'Ah, a letter for you' he announced and tore the envelope open. His sense of propriety was nil. His thirst for information enormous, unlike his member. He was the *Novelist.* To use a cliché, Mira with her heart in her mouth watched him closely, waiting for the laughter to explode but Ritwik after a few millennia like seconds just clutched his heart and sank to the floor. The lethal piece of paper slid out of his long writerly fingers and Mira caught it in mid-flight. It read 'Dear Mrs. Ray, we are delighted to inform....'

ANECDOTAGE

Even at the age of seventy-one Mr. Niyogi gave the impression of corded vigour and vitality. Rather he gave the look of a much younger man. He was tall. His hair gray as steel was thick and brushed back from his wide forehead in a wavy flourish. The teeth too, slightly nicotine stained was still all there.

Every day in the morning he walked for a mile to the post-office and back again. Every so often Mrs. Niyogi would accompany him but after a while she would feel tired and plop down on a bench in the neighbourhood park. Her husband on his way back would pick her up, and then together they would go to the vegetable market, the grocery store and back home to their flat on the fifth floor of a large apartment building in South Delhi.

In contrast to her husband Mrs. Niyogi was tiny, barely touching the five feet mark. Frail and fair, she looked the part of the much loved Bengali grandmother, down to every spunky inch of her diminutive frame.

The Niyogis had one son, Hriday who was a Senior Executive in a foreign bank. Hriday was in some ways the mythical perfect son. Reverent and solicitous and only sometimes mildly critical. He wanted to provide for his parents all the comfort and security he had received when he himself had been a dependent. In this endeavour he was extremely successful but perhaps for this, the real approbrium should go to the lady of the house, Hriday's wife Charu. Who in spite of her busy career as a copy-writer took care of her in-laws as if they were her own parents and never let them feel the neglect which is sadly the lot of most elderly in the autumn of their lives.

On their part the Niyogis gave Hriday and Charu ample breathing space and privacy. They were never meddlesome and only volunteered with an advice when specifically asked for. There were things that they did not like about their son, like his excessive drinking, his late night parties but they never voiced their concern because they knew that the young must live their own lives and that their son was a fine young gentleman, much respected in his own circle and so must be allowed to do his own thing as long as he kept playing tennis in the mornings and generally keep himself fit. Likewise they also felt that Charu was sometimes too strict with her son and most importantly their grandson, Tanmay or Tanu for short. Charu was perpetually worried about her ten year old son's future and the son, though academically bright, was perpetually worried about his batting technique. Whenever Tanu would come home late from the park in the evening he would get a tremendous scolding from his mother but that did not bother him much. He would go and routinely complain to his grandmother, and after wheedling out the requisite sympathy, try to wheedle out some money for comics and succeed every time. Though the Senior Niyogis thought that their bou-ma's behaviour regarding Tanu was a bit obsessive, they wisely kept quiet about it. At night sometimes grandmother Niyogi would say to her husband, 'after all he is her son and the boy does study very little. We must not spoil him.' Mr. Niyogi would nod his head like a sage and look at this simple woman who was his wife for the past forty-five years, his beloved, his strength, his back-bone and feel in his heart love and tenderness of such adolescent intensity that he would pull her towards himself and kiss her full on the lips. She would kiss him back. Then one morning grandma Niyogi died. She had angina pain around midnight but had kept quiet about it, and only when it got unbearable and she was about to lose her consciousness, did she wake Mr. Niyogi up. It was too late by then. She died couple of hours later in the ICU of a reputed nursing home.

The son lost his mother, Charu that rare commodity: a

loving mother-in-law and young Tanu his 'Bank' but Mr. Niyogi as good as forfeited his life. The shock of her absence was simply too much to bear for this retired Don of literature, late of Patna University. Keats and his 'Ode to a Nightingale' became his theme. He lost his will to live and wished each night that life should curl up into an iron ball and roll out of him. For old Mr. Niyogi, to whom once Byron was the greatest of all the 'Romantics', and whose reading of *Don Juan* was attended by packed class rooms, young men and women imbibing from his lips the vitality which flowed from Byron to him in a continuous stream, now only had ears for the tender strains of the ever melancholic Keats. In Keat's lush lachrymose lines, his loneliness found a voice and in the evenings he invariably sat with a volume of the great man's poems.He did not venture out anymore. Sometimes he would go to the market place but even so little an exertion would put him out of breath. He did not say much to anyone but all watched his condition with growing trepidation. Hriday and Charu would relay to each other their growing fear that 'Baba is literally willing himself to die', every night but even discussing the conundrum for a whole night, no solution would be forthcoming at dawn.

Tanu too watched his dadu with curiosity and he could not fathom how so much of effervescence could suddenly revert into a tower of silence. He did not like this silent, morose dadu, who would not even discuss with him the ever fluctuating fortunes of the Indian cricket team or the latest catchy Hindi film song or whether his English 'miss' was prettier than Kajol? While the earlier dadu – ah, he was something else. He was fun. But even Tanu would sometimes catch the sadness in the air and on those days he would not go out to play but sit with his dadu quietly. He prayed that his dadu should return to his old playful persona. He prayed that his grandfather should smile again. And he said to God one day in exasperation, 'Just make him snap out of it, will you? Enough is enough!'

But it is never enough. Mr. Niyogi could not get enough of sadness. He did not pity himself, he did not damn God but he did crave for ever more sadness. He punished himself for all the happiness that had come his way and he wanted his body and mind purged of all the laughter, the good times, love, the memory of his wife, her voice, her smell, her body.

The epicure started starving himself. He started keeping random fasts. He abstained from his mandatory glass of scotch which earlier Mrs. Niyogi used to fix for him every evening before dinner. He threw away all the pouches of expensive pipe tobacco that Hriday regularly brought for him, and, on top of it all, one day he even stopped eating fish! He pushed the dish away from himself with a feeble hand, the sight of the clean white flesh in a yellow rich gravy of mustard made his face visibly pale with nausea. Charu could not stop her tears, Hriday just shook his head very slowly, and Tanu's chin hit his chest on a downward curve and stayed there for the rest of the meal.

The memory of Mrs. Niyogi clung to him like a fine mist. He never could shake out of it, it chilled his spirit of all vitality but it was also a comfort to him in a languishing sort of way. He remembered the time he first saw her, on their wedding night, in the mandap, realising how tiny and fragile she was, like a bird made of porcelain. Her eyes kohl rimmed looking up to his with a bold impishness and her muffled cries of pain as they made love for the first time. The pain of her penetration brought tears to the eyes of Mr. Niyogi forty-five years later. Back then it had only brought pleasure.

The hair started thinning over the top making his pink scalp peek out in despair. The skin too looked thin and papery and one day he asked Hriday to bring him a good walking stick.

At night when all were asleep he would close his room, remove all his clothes and stand nude before Mrs. Niyogi's dressing table and look at his reflection with a critic's eye for detail. He would then run his hand over his now sunken belly, the thin hairless legs, over the muscles that had lost their definition, the hollow cheeks, and wrinkled neck, the spare pubic hair and would cup his balls, the size of grapes hanging loose in their wafer thin sacs, almost transparent and he would look with profound satisfaction at the startling metamorphosis he had achieved in only a couple of months time. He would then intone loudly. 'At my back I always hear / time's winged chariot hurrying near' and wake Hriday and Charu sleeping in the next room, without fail.

He never used the walking stick. It remained propped against the dressing table and once in a while Mr. Niyogi would pick it up and swing it around like a sword when he thought no one was looking in but twice Tanu caught him and promptly reported the matter to Charu, who thought wisely of saying nothing to her husband. It seems that some amount of vanity still remained embedded in the old bones. Thus all was not lost. Till there is vanity, there is hope.

Six months after the death things began to change. The weather started to clear. Life still seemed like a burden to Mr. Niyogi but he had started reading the cricket scores again. He started talking with Tanu again and would listen patiently to his animated patter about school life.

When his old cronies would come, he did not shoo them away like before but offered them tea and sympathy and listened to their cynical diatribe about family life. Scotch and tobacco were still taboo. Ditto with fish.

Then one day in the afternoon, for the first time in so many months, he went up the staircase to the roof of his apartment building. When Mrs. Niyogi had been alive, they had always strolled together, hand in hand, Mrs. N chirping away continuously, each evening.

That day as he walked into the open air surroundings, he felt fresh and clean and he was not thinking about his beloved anymore. He was not thinking about anything. He felt at ease with the world and miraculously he did not feel guilty about it anymore. He stopped by the side of the flower pots and looked at the flowers in full bloom, the marigolds, the daisies, dahlias and some long stemmed burgundy roses and they gave him the same lush pleasure as before. He walked round, looking at the neighbouring buildings, the diminutive people walking on the streets below and suddenly he noticed a familiar figure in the corner on the other side of the apartment building.

It was young Tanu, totally lost in himself, looking at something with rapt attention on the other side, over the edge, standing a little away from the railing. Mr. Niyogi was surprised to see Tanu because by that time, usually, he was out playing cricket in the park.

Intrigued, he too went and stood behind Tanu and peered over the edge. The boy did not notice anything, such was his concentration. In the next building, in a top floor bathroom, a magnificent young women was taking a shower. Her strong firm flesh seemed moulded out of white porcelain. The sight of it was like a hot white light in Mr. Niyogi's eyes. It blinded him for a second. His faculties starved so long for beauty were sharper now for the neglect. Like an adolescent he felt as if he had discovered the beauty of the female form for the first time in his life.

Then memory fed him the sensual images of his beloved, which he to himself had denied for so long. The image and the reality collapsed into one another and became one. For a second, he felt like a dirty old man but the next moment he felt gloriously alive and strangely enough, in a flash, a line from a classic Jibanananda Das poem came to his lips in a silent prayer: '... and a touch of peace came to me/once the tiredest of all men/the gift of a village-girl of natore/Banalata Sen.' He watched her for sometime in complete silence and then he gently tapped the kid on the shoulder.

'Do you know who that is, son?' And Tanu, startled, red-faced looked at his grandfather in fear, sure now that he was in the worst jam of his short career as a bird-watcher. 'I do not know what you are talking about.' He tried to get away but Mr. Niyogi caught him and made him look at the girl again, now toweling herself in a languid manner. 'The girl, look at the girl, do you know her name? Because if you do not, you must.' And Mr. Niyogi laughed his full throated laughter the first time in months.

'No, I do not know her name. 'Tanu said, eyes downcast, still red-faced.

'She is Banalata Sen, my son. She is Banalata Sen.'

'Come on dadu, she is not a Bengali, she is Dolly Makhija, my friend Andy's sister.' Tanu tried to put the matter straight.'So, you do know her name?'

'The whole colony does.' Tanu replied making his stand clear.

'No more of this from tomorrow, one must take one's cricket very seriously.'

'Yes dadu, but you wont tell ma, would you?'

'Of course not.' Mr. Niyogi said and gave Tanu a reassuring wink.

And Tanu made a mental note to congratulate God on a job well done.

Hand in hand grandfather-grandson walked down the stairs to the flat, where Tanu started practising square cuts in front of the mirror.

Mr. Niyogi lit his pipe, put the volume of Keats back into the almirah and took out his much thumbed copy of *Don Juan* and held its brittle sepia-toned pages to the light which suddenly seemed to have flooded the room.

RIVER OF DREAMS

I am going back. I can't work anymore. Each day, it is getting harder and harder to breathe. All the fields must be green and really beautiful by now and the sweet scent of rain and soft kneaded black soil would be in the air and the small ponds all filled up and the canals too, and I know, right this moment all of them are snaking in and diving and splashing like silver brown fishes in the water, playing with the dung encrusted buffalows who roam near the water banks of the pond and a little later when the sun goes down and the pale moon comes to watch over us, they will be near the railway tracks throwing pebbles and running alongside the evening trains which pass through the village like strangers, without a sideways glance or a tender smile, in complete detachment of rapid monotonous motion. I wish I was with them, near the tracks. The tracks feel so cool and lonely in the evenings, and when you put your ear to it you can hear the rumblings of its ancient soul echoing the future that will be past us in a few quick minutes. My mother would be making the evening meal in front of our hut, her head covered with her sari and bent over the stove and smoke from the dungfuel making eyes burn. Every once in a while she would wipe her watery eyes and stare into the disappearing darkness and call breathlessly 'Ram, Ram .... Ram, come home son.'

Ram came to work for us around 4 or 5 months back and for days I barely noticed him. He was of a very slight build, very quite and used to jump when the phone used to ring. Later on when I came to know that he was 14 years old I was surprised; he didn't look more than 10 or 11 to me. I guess something deep inside him was pulling him down, wasn't allowing him to grow. He was thin, really thin, all his ribs could be counted easily – but he ate okay, in fact he ate too much and his hair stood on his head like spikes on a steel coat brush, and one thing more, he barely ever smiled. His uncle who was 2 or 3 years older than me and who used to work for us for a long time and was now married and had two kids of his own, brought Ram to our place because, I guess, they really needed the money and feeding him in the village was burning a big hole in their budget. But he refused to do any work. 'He roams around the village like an idiot and his mother fears that he will drown one day or be crushed under some speeding train.' His uncle informed my mother. This uncle of Ram is a real piece of work, around the same time, the plague scare broke out all over Patna and do you know what he did? Ofcourse you don't. he tied an old Tomcat on a string and went visiting the scared rich all over town to ferret out rats and killing them for a fee – and you now what? I think he carried with himself a ready supply of rats too, caught from the gutters! He is one hell of an enterprising man. He charged Rs. 25 per kill and in a week he had made over Rs. 1000 in cold hard cash. Now they are saying it wasn't caused by the rats at all but, as far as Munna (Ram's uncle) is concerned, the plague was just fine; it should come at least once each year.

At Rs. 500/- a month, Ram was taken in and his job was to clean and wash and dust, help mother with the cooking and generally do everything that was asked of him. He barely said anything ever, and whenever he did it was with such a thick 'over the ganges' accent that it was hard to make out what he said anyway. Everything surprised him: the phone, the doorbell, the elevator, which I suppose was the only thing that really delighted him in those first few weeks, and he would go up and down again up and press all the buttons and be generally happy in that enclosed area of his freedom. But then one day another small servant of a neighbouring flat in our building got stuck in the elevator and after that everybody became apprehensive what if their own beautiful brat angels got stuck instead? I am sure the thought must have pierced their hearts like a sabre. So a 'Bill' was passed that no small children or servants should use the elevator unchaperoned. So, that was that, but a ride in there till the end remained a thing of wonder and joy for him. The T.V. became another of his pleasures and after finishing work and later on even between the chores, he would go and sit in front of the screen and watch everything with a brightness in his eyes that was missing at other times and sometimes in the silence of the afternoon when everything would be still in the oppressive heat of Patna, I would catch him solemnly sitting crosslegged in front of the unlit T.V. and on the screen nothing except thin film of dust – totally blank – but there Ram would be sitting like the proverbial buddha under the bodhi tree. I just couldn't figure it out.

In the afternoon my friends would come and then we would all go out barefooted into the fields of mustard, feeling the black moist soil with our soles wading through acres of the green yellow land and on to the canal where we would ride the bullocks into the muddy waters and then dive with eyes closed and long fingers clasping the nose and sink down into the brown spreading softness. They will laugh at me if they ever find out what I really do out here, if they ever find out that I wash and clean the clothes and do the cooking like the girls instead of working as a fruit seller as I have told them, I will die of shame. I won't ever go back to the village but what will I do? I can't stay here, I can't even breathe this foul air, sometimes when I breathe I can't even exhale, the air inside contracting my lungs, choking me. I can't sleep and all night the wheel turns overhead and one day it will fall ....

A week or two after his arrival, one day, I noticed him picking up the phone when it rang and after a few seconds he hurriedly put it down as if it were some repulsive reptile. I was surprised that he had even picked up the phone because he wasn't supposed to, but on the other hand, I had always noticed the expression of intense curiosity on his face whenever the phone used to ring. 'What happened, Ram?' I called out to him. He turned towards me slowly, his eyes were again its dull fused-bulb natural self but his mouth was slightly open, his nostrils flared and the hair on his head stood like millions of bright black needles. He looked positively angry. 'What happened? Why did you....' 'He knows me, he calls out to me.' He said slowly and I realised then that he wasn't angry or any thing but just confused and perhaps a little scared that a strange green contraption could curl up around your ear like a snake and blow weird sounds from nothingness like 'Hello Ram?' Later on in the day I came to know that father had called up from his office and recognising Ram's voice had uttered his name and Ram had put the receiver down; even my father was confused. He thought may be he had got the wrong number. I tired in vain to explain the way the phone works to Ram but something told me, perhaps from the look of total distrust in his eyes he wasn't much convinced – he probably thought it was possessed by the devil or something. He didn't go near the phone for a long time after that. But he smartened up quickly and would spend much time in front of the mirror trying to flatten his punk style hair-do much to my mother's exasperation. My mother found him to be infinitely lazy – his ability for doing nothing all day was just awesome – and she was right too, because he was always listless and would dust a single stretch of window panes for hours or at any given opportunity disappear into the toilet and stay there for half an hour at a stretch. God knows what he did in there! No amount of scolding could make him see the light. He would, in the evening, stand in the balcony and stare at the stretching sky and keep on staring, his long fingers gripping the iron railing, though, mind you, sometimes the sky would be as bare, starless, devoid of light like the unlit T.V. set. But he would still keep on staring at it, charting, perhaps, the course of his uncertain life through the unknown sky. Some people wish upon a star but maybe his dreams were hinged on nothingness or maybe he just didn't have anything better to do. But at those times I almost admired him, his innate ability to stay aloof from everything although deep down inside I just couldn't figure it out. I was four years elder to him and on a whim I tired to make him study. He was literate, he knew the alphabets all right, he could write his own name but his interest died right there. Language, literature, education had no use for him, as far as he was concerned. It was futile trying to educate him, he would look listlessly around and one day he literally dozed off right in the middle of a lesson – so much for education and my humble efforts. But Ram was all right in a way, I guess. Once he caught me smoking in my room, well he didn't catch me or anything but the just barged into my room (he didn't care much about knocking), and there I was sprawled on my bed with pillows stacked high celebrating my few hours of freedom (my parents had gone to a party), the stereo blowing *River of Dreams* and smoke slowly curling away from the lit cigarette in my hand, but I made him promise not to tell and he kept the promise (he had come in because he liked the song, he informed me and stood there listening to Billy Joel's sweet cool voice, and when the song ended he went away, without a backward glance. He had integrity I must admit, and in return I would turn on the T.V. for him when there would be no one at home.

Here at night even the stars don't shine, they are like small bulbs in the sky which go on and off into the darkness but in my village the stars look so big and bright and happy watching over us and showing us the way through the fields and into woods shining through the yellow green leaves of the mango trees but here all is indifference, even the moon forgets to look beautiful and comes out unwashed and ugly. At nights I lie awake in the darkness and hear frogs croak near the pond and sweet night sounds of my village which lull me to sleep sometimes but when dawn arrives I am still here, trapped, and there is no escape.

Sometimes I would send him out to fetch me cigarettes and he would dash off in a hurry as if he were a mouse released from the mousetrap and I would watch him from the balcony, negotiate his way cautiously through the heavy afternoon traffic, slow and diffident amidst the rush, his walk incongrous on the hot black coaltar street, his foot going clomp clomp clomp as if he were walking in the soft mud soil of the wet rice fields of his beloved village (whose beauty he sometimes described to me), instead. I guess I had won his trust and I trusted him too so it came as a real shock when he finally did what he did.

Everything is slipping away slowly from my memory and like the train slowly leaving the station and people receding into the background like trivial dots, I am slipping away going down into the darkness, my home, my mother, the little lemon shrub which my father had planted before he went away, everything is slowly slipping away like these white delicate tea cups that I am rinsing under the tap, they too float away and crash and burn shatter in the sink of my dreams. Did you hear the crash? Tell me can you listen to my heart? CAN YOU HEAR AT ALL? ANSWER ME YOU. …

Couple of weeks back I reached home around 8 in the evening after hanging out with my friends for a few hours at the market place, smoking and telling jokes and whistling at the girls, and they looking at us from beneath their shining eyes, looking cool and unaffected, the backslapping, eyewinking, elbow nudging rites of our innocence, and generally had a great time. I am at my happiest when I am with my friends doing what everyone else is doing – nothing. My mother and a lady who lives in the flat across were standing outside our flat. My mother looked a bit flustered to me. 'He is not opening the door,' My mother said to me. 'Who's inside?' 'Why do you always ask such foolish questions Ritwik, Ram is not opening the door.'

'Why?'

'Why? I don't know why.'

'What happened really?'

'Half an hour ago I went to the terrace and told him to lock the door and that I will be back soon and now he is not opening the door and he has got the T.V. on too.'

My mother was correct, as usual. I could hear the faint strains of wild guitar riffs coming from inside and started to bang the door loudly but to no avail.

'He is insolent and lazy he just won't listen to anything I say. Today he also broke my precious tea set, all the twelve cups and saucers. I just could not believe it and last week he smashed my flower vase, this is deliberate cruelty. I got angry and really scolded him hard but he just stood there like a tomcat amidst trashcans, indolent and slouching. I don't know what to do with him and now he is sitting in there, watching T.V.' My mother said to the lady who wagged her head in a dutiful manner.

'He is watching M.T.V.'

'Does it matter what he is watching Ritwik, I have been standing outside for the past 10 minutes, so do something constructive for the first time in your life.' My mother was all worked up and I, must admit, was getting a bit worried too. Strange thoughts started coming into my head like what if he smashed my stereo or tore apart all my precious books out of rancour, God, I would die. I love my stereo or may be my stash of *Fantasy, Debonair, Fun*, which he knew I kept underneath the mattress, oh my God, what to do? I rang the bell and kept it pressed till it ran out of steam and whined faintly. 'Perhaps he has hurt himself'. The lady suggested to my mother. Now my mother was really worried. Other people, neighbours and assorted strangers started showing their really concerned faces around our door and advices started pouring in like thick rain drops.

I went downstairs and called my father, the matter was getting out of control and I realised I was no good in a crisis situation. I am a civilian, I belong in the peace time. My father said he would rush back quickly was back within 20 minutes, and by that time mother was reduced to tears and I don't know why some of the other ladies too were dabbing their eyes with their hankies, children and one small dog also there, playing and howling (the brats were playing and the dog was howling), and I almost lost my mind and for the first time in my life. I felt my brain melt and evaporate into nothingless. I felt so empty that I stopped sensing anything and just went and sat down on the stairs – detached from the chaos, staring at the dog. He was a small brown mongrel with a real sweet sad expression on his face. Perhaps he was going crazy too. … I am sure even he wasn't there by his own choice and like myself would have much preferred to have been elsewhere – anywhere infact. My father suggested we break open the door and everybody enthusiastically consented. Somehow we managed to break it open and my father and I rushed inside. Everything was still and silent and dark as no light was on anywhere except for a thin ray of light that came from the sitting room mixed with faint echoes of rockmusic. We pushed open the door, At first we couldn't see anything as the room was dark and the only light that came was from the flickering T.V. screen. Ram was lying on the carpet face upwards staring steadily into nothingness. There was no movement in this body and for a second I thought that he was dead. He turned his head slowly towards us, saw us, and I am sure we must have looked pretty ridiculous standing there. Then he started laughing – really wild and out of control – I tried to calm him down before my father did something terrible to him, but he hit me across my face and grabbed me; there was so much strength in those thin arms, a low scream like a call of a trapped small animal in great pain came out from him and big tears came streaming down his face. Father tried to free us but he just hung on to me by my shirt front and in the end my new T-shirt was ripped to pieces. I looked into his eyes for the last time. He was sent away right then and there with our driver back to his village. Why did he do it? He had everything here, I mean I just couldn't understand it at that time. A week later Munna came by, said he was sad but that everything would be all right and the very next day he brought another of his proteges; this time a cousin of his. So everything is fine now and life goes on as usual. Everybody acts as if nothing has happened and I guess it is fine by me too. But still when I am alone sometimes, sitting and brooding in my room at night, I can feel his long fingers grabbing and tearing my T-shirt and the look in his eyes, a look of rage mixed with helplessness, anger dipped in tears, a kind of betrayal, yes, that's what it was, the look of complete betrayal – that moaning shrill low scream of pain violates my ears like thin sharp needles and goes on and on and on until I can't take it anymore. I crawl on my knees to my stereo and put on some rockmusic and pump up the volume to the limit to drown out his scream and more often than not I play *River of Dreams.*

DIKSHA AT ST. MARTIN'S

Let me warn you at the outset, Scorsese to me is God. A tiny (5 feet nothing) private God whose image I carry locked in my heart, ready for an impromptu worship anywhere at the drop of a cigarette butt. He is my own private personal Ganesh. The conflict ridden God of good and bad tidings both. A source of hope and inspiration at all times.

Growing up in the late eighties in the tough Bihari- Bengali neighbourhood of Kadam Kuan; Patna, I saw *Mean Streets* for the first time and immediately recognized those streets, the milieu, those small time 'wiseguys' to be mine. The streets, galis and nukkads of little Italy, New York seemed superimposed on the parallel ones of Kadam Kuan. So that afternoon, at age fourteen I got my 'diksha' from St. Martin in a rickety scabrous illegal video parlour with wooden schoolroom benches to sit on and such poor acoustics that one never got the dialogues ever. In time one learnt to lip-read or perchance blessed with imagination, made up the dialogues themselves. I had simply learnt to switch off my ears whenever I went there and in a sense all the movies I saw there were silent ones. Only the images remain stuck to my mind like postage stamps. So only 'moving pictures', which actually 'moved', had any impact in such trying circumstances. Merchant - Ivory could have died and gone to heaven and nobody there would have noticed. Ditto with St. Martin's *The Age of Innocence* (1993), one of the few chipped clay toes of my God.

15 minutes into the movie and the audience had thinned out. Most of the 'gentry' cursing Ghoshda for showing a movie, which was 'ekdam faltu' (meaning nobody yet had fucked their brains out on the screen), and had walked out. It was a miracle Ghoshda didn't get shot, people had died for much less in Kadam Kuan. For Ghoshda it was the year of living dangerously and the very next week he showed *Apocalypse Now*! God bless him. The video parlour closed down the next year and Ghosh da opened a 'chinize' food joint which the 'gentry' again ruined it for him by congregating there each evening. He now runs a cyber café at the same spot.

Back to *Mean Streets*. For the first time in my life I was watching something close to my own reality (perhaps at that very moment a young boy in Bolton or Vermont watching the Apu trilogy was feeling the same) and which from cinema I had never got before. From the opening drum beats of the Ronettes *Be my baby* to the shootout at the end (Scorsese himself putting in a cameo as the diminutive hitman, Shorty). It was the attitude that said 'coolness is all' grabbed me by my bandana (I was a frightful little punk those days) and dragged me into a world so unlike my own yet so recognizable, so immediate. The petty crooks and extortionists, the grassroot level political activists, small time scamsters and dreamers, the camaraderie and the little betrayals. People getting born and dying in the same place, never venturing out for more than a thirty minute distance from their homes in their entire lives. The quiet desperation of young men with limited education and choices for whom aping the ways and lifestyle of a mythic local 'Rangbaz' of the moment seemed infinitely more profitable than finishing college and getting jobs. Well, there were not many jobs in Patna anyway. For them a simple nod from that self same Rangbaz, something or the other 'da' would make their days completely memorable. That nod would give them identity and add swagger to their walk. After the nod would come a pat on the back, next the handshake and the katta would change hands. A diksha of a different kind. There would be no going back then. Their glory would last a few months, a year at the most till some younger kid with more desperation and less to lose would come and end their misery. A single shot at the back of the head while pissing at the street corner, one warm Sunday evening.

The Godfather was mythology. This was real life. The garish orangish redlights of the nightclubs and the intensity of the fist fights, which actually looked like fist fights, not some synchronized ballet, where the people had hands which were 'open' (Haanth Khola) and actually took their time, aimed and hit the face. The thing about a fight is that you must always hit first, your hands shouldn't ever be like those of Hamlet's (they must be open and quick), because in a little while (a minute), people would come and try to break-up the fight anyway. Never slap because that wouldn't do any damage, adding to the fact that it would be an insult, making it more dangerous in the long run. Also do not call anyone a 'mook'. Ever. The suddenness of the fights erupting over trivial matters, the macho honour thing, over somebody's sister (Ritwik's fucking her, I want my share too. Fuck Ritwik), over street corners (I saw Ritwik pissing against your pole. Fuck Ritwik) over a cup of tea, over not being offered a charminar gratis by the paanwallah (Fuck Ritwik anyway!).

Instant connection. In Johnny boy's (Robert De Niro), almost psychotic irresponsibility I could see the reflection of a childhood friend who even then I knew would turn out to be trouble (he was shot a couple of years later grabbing booths, by the police in Danapore). Birju survived but now has one foot couple of inches shorter than the other and which he props up like a trophy on a table which is kept specially for him infront of the cyber café, as each evening he holds forth on the future course of Lalooland. The boys who sit listening to him awestruck, staring enviously at the stump ordering tea and charminar, get younger and younger each year. They graduate and go away but my friend sits there each evening, reworking his stories, finding new narratives, adding lines, deleting some, his only concern being 'will it be good for charminars and a cup of tea next season when the new batch enrolls'. Diksha again. But perhaps then he sees his stump, pats it lovingly and feels reassured. Like a beggar he knows the stump is his meal ticket. Until the day a man with a eye patch as well as a gimp fades in through the mist my friend needn't lose his sleep.

If the *The Godfather* (1972) in an ironic way was about family values, then *Mean Streets* (1973) set a couple of decades later is about the neighbourhood, the 'mohallah' or 'para', a tale of growing up, a tale of friendships, of not fucking up, about survival and responsibility. An intensely autobiographical movie, which Pauline Kael in her landmark review furthering the cause of the yet unknown Scorsese called 'a triumph of personal film making'. In a mohallah, one is responsible for everything, for oneself, for the family, for friends, because there is no getting away from it. It is part of the culture. One imbibes it just by breathing. It is like living in a constant fish bowl. The individual doesn't matter, the community or the group does. Charlie (Harvey Keitel) weighed down by Catholic guilt (incidentally Scorsese wanted to become a priest when he was in his teens), realizes that. He can't disown his friend (though conventional wisdom suggests he should), Johnny boy even though he knows that the kid is bad news, will foul up big and get him into even more trouble and jeopardize all his plans of upward mobility. But one doesn't abandon a friend because he will bring trouble (friends are bound to do that anyway). The code doesn't allow that. One is implicated by association. Look what happened to poor George (not of the Jungle but from a similar place). There is no getting away from it. Charlie knows it and he realizes that Johnny boy is his responsibility and he has to look out for him. Johnny is one of those 18 till I die fellows who till the time they are alive cause any number of trouble for all concerned. We have all had friends or relatives like that, and there is little one can do about it except hope for the best, that he will settle down after marriage and instead wreck some poor simple minded young woman's life who has had the singular misfortune to get hitched to him. Generally it has been noted, things work out fine after that.

Charlie is answerable for Johnny boy's refusal to pay back Michael the loanshark (Richard Romanus in a standout performance), and in the end will pay dearly for it. Johnny would never realize it and if he survives would do the same thing again. Like the scorpion he just can't change his nature. He has no sense of responsibility and is the eternal younger brother. In many ways, it is the story of two brothers, with all its attendant jealousies, rivalries, concern, and care. A theme to which Scorsese would return again in *Raging Bull* (1980), in his portrayal of the La Motta brothers (Pesci and De Niro) and in *Casino* (1996) where Ace Rothstein (De Niro) and Nicky Santoro (Joe Pesci) play childhood friends turned enemies. If Charlie and Johnny boy survive into maturity they would perhaps turn into Rothstein and Santoro of the later movie. The one always in control, the other unpredictable and violent. Women are incidental in most of Scorsese movies (notable exceptions being *Alice doesn't live here anymore* (1979), and *The Age of Innocence* (1993), and one more chipped clay toe *New York, New York* (1977). What they do is basically light the fuse. Cathy Moriarty's bitch goddess in *Raging Bull*, Betsy (Cybil Shepard) the uptown cock- tease in *Taxi driver* (1976), and the confused high class hooker Ginger (Sharon Stone), of *Casino*. Even in *Mean Streets* the one woman character, Charlie's epileptic girlfriend Teresa (Amy Robinson), is under fleshed, though it brings out the tender side of his personality and whom he would probably give up because, according to the resident 'wise guy' Uncle Giovanni (Cesare Denova), she is not right 'in the head', thus cursed by God and what's more 'honourable men should go with honourable men'. Marrying her wouldn't further Charlie's ambition of breaking into the inner circle of the mafia and becoming a ' made guy'.

Charlie is in many ways a conformist, alternatively heroic and weak, an upwardly mobile lower middle class man who just wants enough so he could live with dignity and enter his own home justified each night to a loving wife and a bambino or two. In the end he too wants to settle down, to put down roots and be a perfect representative of the bourgeois class and attend PTA meetings. Years later, just before he got shot and acquired legendary status, Birju pandey and I were sitting in a tea shop near Hathwa market eyeing the girls when suddenly he had a joycean epiphanic moment as an exquisitely beautiful girl in a chiffon sari chattering in Bengali passed us by with her mother. Pandey turned and looked at me and said 'You know what I really want in life, I want a wife who goes to kitty parties'. He could have been joking but I wouldn't put my money on it. Like his brethren in little Italy he too knew that the inherent futility of dreams shouldn't ever stop one from dreaming them.

It is not a easy movie to watch. You can't do it while flipping a magazine or having 'Chinize' food. Scorsese isn't Spielberg. He demands your undivided attention and more often than not you give it willingly. Those who can't have no option but to leave, like all those friends and neighbours of mine who had walked into the showing of *Mean Streets* thinking it to be an 'adult movie'. Unfortunately they were all underage. I was to witness a similar situation in Delhi in 1996 during a matinee of *Casino* at Priya. There were a lot of miffed girlfriends angrily sucking on a soda during intermission while the boyfriends looked funked out, not knowing what had hit them. Scorsese is bit of an endurance test; moreover he doesn't take kindly to ignorance.

Now a word of advice: If you are going out to pay your respect to St. Martin, leave the girlfriend at the altar. She might love the movie (a long shot), but on the other hand, why take the chance? The saint ain't easy on relationships either. He is married five times over and probably still hasn't got it right. Two more and Liz Taylor would start feeling threatened. While De Niro's high octane portrayal is something to behold (Coppola saw this performance during post production and immediately cast De Niro as the calm and controlled Vito Corleone in *The Godfather-II* (1974), which incidentally won him a best supporting actor Oscar), Keitel another Scorsese regular (he has made six movies with him right from the time of his first feature *Who is That Knocking at My Door* (1968), is dignified, compassionate and in the end heroic, anchoring the screenplay with his presence and giving it the requisite solidity. De Niro's is the explosive, flashier performance but it is Harvey Keitel, a.k.a. Mr. *Bad Lieutenant* (another gem of a movie with strong catholic overtones), who is the actual revelation of the film. The screenplay by Scorsese and Mardik Martin is as tightly sewn as a baseball and the influence of its 'chatty' style on Tarantino's, *Pulp Fiction* (1994), is all too evident. *Mean Streets* was the breakthrough movie for all the three concerned, Scorsese, De Niro and Keitel and made their bones and their reputations in Hollywood. As I walked out drenched in sweat from the parlour in the evening, the shirt unbuttoned, the bandana around my neck dripping wet, I probably looked like someone who had just run a marathon and still had the crazy bright gleam in the eye; testosterone kicking in constantly. In many ways, that afternoon I had run a marathon of the mind and had left my surroundings, my friends, far behind. The Video parlour had a tin roof. A hot tin roof. I was the cat who jumped off it and kept on moving, past my friends at the park playing cricket, past some 'da's' at the teashop, who as usual called after me but I didn't hear them anymore. I had switched off my ears again. Years later when I was 18 and had suddenly decided to be a writer, I would write my first short story with St. Martin as a motif, which the *Sunday Observer* in 1993 serialized for six weeks. The story was called 'Any Fan of Martin Scorsese is a friend of mine', and you know what mate, the title still holds true.